INDIA IN THE CROSSHAIRS is a wonderful book of Wisdom! Kip "Kipacharya" Finn's love for Dharma is a divine gift. The author exhorts Indians: *"Bharat, quit running after your neighbors. We all want what you have and come great distances at considerable expense to get just a little taste of it. You are a unique nation. Be proud of your accomplishments..."*

Acharya Kip's advice, that India should remember and embrace her spiritual heritage and tradition by putting Dharma first and individual desires second is to be followed by Indians in practice. No use of boasting, bragging and blustering on Dharma and live self deceitful lives. Practice not prattle!!

Dr.Rao.. M.D.
Rao Ayurvedic Clinic
Puttaparti, Andra Pradesh, India

INDIA IN THE
CR⊕SSHAIRS

An American Perspective

Kipacharya
KIP FINN

POCO LOCO

INDIA IN THE
CR✛SSHAIRS
An American Perspective

First Edition 2007

Co-published by:
Message Publications
23/1142, Vijayalakshmi Colony, Kadugudi
Bangalore 560 067

United States: 393-7585
Contact the author at *kipacharya@yahoo.com*
or visit *www.kipfinn.com*

A catalogue record for this book is available from the British Library.

Typeset in 10.5 pt Garamond
Titles in 16pt Imprint MT Shadow

ISBN 978-81-86822-80-1

Cover design by Mohan Kumar K.R.

Printed and bound in India by
Vishruti Prints

Table of Contents

Thank You for Joining Me

In 2005 when O.P. Khanna invited me to address the International Rotary Club in Bangalore, the I.T. capital of India, my heart skipped a beat. Fully trusting that if the skipping continued, Khanna, Coordinator, the Feely Heart Foundation at Manipal Hospital would broker my healthcare, I accepted. At the time I had been traveling extensively through India so I titled the talk *From Badrinath To Kanyakumari: A Westerner's Perspective.* In the course of my travels I had amassed a pile of notes and decided to not only give a travel log but also present the membership with a transcription of those notes as published articles.

India In The Crosshairs is somewhat of a misnomer, even though blasting Bangalore seems to be a pet peeve. The turret of my tongue is often aimed at the city, with many of the sarcastic articles targeting the leadership. Bangalore, an emerging modern metropolis, is used symbolically to represent India in general – the 'fall guy'– and my Western perspective of your Eastern culture. Also, for every complaint I've offered a solution – *cheese* is served with the *whine*. Those of us who live here, even part-time, love this eclectic city which contributes much to the nation and the world. It is an epicenter of change, pregnant with potential – I just wonder who the father is?!

These articles have already produced complaints – proud citizens of a great nation upset at being ridiculed. I've discovered things that shock me don't have the same impact on you, and if it's any consolation, I'm sorry for stepping on toes. However, if East and West are going to 'do it', only by sharing impressions and exchanging ideas can our intercourse be smooth. Like I told one young reader, particularly upset with the article *Pissing In Public:* "It's only an opinion. And, like a certain organ of elimination – we all have one!"

When I finished reading Abdul Kalam's first book, *Wings Of Fire*, I wrote a powerful piece of music titled, *Bharat I Believe*. After reading *Ignited Minds* I contacted the head of the Engineering and Applied Technology Dept at one of the country's most prestigious universities and shared some alternate energy ideas with his students. It's an exciting time to live in India. The President envisions the nation achieving fully developed status within a generation—which means everyone will have to do their jobs with more *thrust!* Everywhere you look are 'scoring opportunities in a target rich environment' – ways to make money; ways to improve society, ways to develop.

As an observer I've been blessed to see incredible things—saints and sages, palaces, places of pilgrimage, fertile fields, tea plantations, wild elephants, peacocks dancing on the Ganga banks. The beauty of this land is phenomenal. Likewise, there is an evasive attraction – the antiquity, the wisdom teachings, the novelty and uniqueness – that draws people from all over the world. Somewhere between Uttar Pradesh and Karnataka came a revelation: *You don't have to be a citizen of India to be a son or daughter*. Her children are everywhere.

I am an American, but I like to remember what Prime Minister Manmohan Singh said to India's little brother, Pakistan, "The world requires we have borders, but we can choose to act like they do not exist…" And though our borders are well demarcated and an ocean separates us, the distance between India and America is rapidly narrowing in the confluence of our cultures.

Namaste, mera dost

Kip "Kipacharya" Finn
23/1142, Vijayalakshmi Colony, Kadugodi, Bangalore, April 2007

৵৵

Bharat, I Believe

Dedicated to Abdul Kalam

We found a way to navigate the night
Dispel the darkness with a little light
Against the gods; against all odds
Together our sweet dream came true

The first couplet is the *Asatoma* prayer; the 'gods' represent the forces of nature and political powers. Of course, this was Kalam's dream—for *Bharat* (India)—to build its own indigenous missiles and rockets. Very few nationals believed they had the capability.

We found a way to climb to the stars
They tried denying what was always ours
A working team realized the dream
Oh, Bharat, I Believe in you

The team's dream was to put a satellite in outer space and when India put *Rohini* into orbit, she became the sixth nation in the world to achieve this incredible feat. Kalam, who inspired this song, coordinated the efforts of 200 scientists and a huge private and government complex to 'realize the dream'.

We found a way no one would have guessed
Before a nation we soared to success
The stakes were high; to do or die
I never stopped believing you

When India announced its success the G-8 imposed sanctions against her and each accused the other of providing the technology. The hero of the story forfeited marriage, children, hearth and home. Kalam lived in a one-room apartment for over twenty years, and dedicated his entire waking moments to his two great loves – *Bharat* and science.

The sculptor's hammer reveals the precious stone
Explorers sailing into the unknown
Before the cheers we shed some tears
Right from the start, in my heart
Oh, Bharat, I Believe in you

The *sculptor*—God—revealing the *gemstone*—the best in Man through refinement—is a classical metaphor. This tribute to *Bharat* is written from Kalam's perspective, who also happens to be a fine Tamil poet. Great challenges demand superlative responses and indefatigable spirit. Imagine the disappointment of working five years continuously then watching your nation's first space vehicle have to be destroyed only 200 seconds after the launch. More than tears were shed; hearts were broken—but Kalam carried on, never quitting or questioning. Why? Because: *Bharat, I Believe in you...*

A Letter Home
Part 1

Dear Brother: I have found a niche for myself here in India. I was thinking that perhaps you'd like to visit but want to prepare you first. It is so different from our father's home in California. If you're afraid of hard work you wouldn't like it here; unlike us who put in a leisurely 8/5 the people here work 10/6—10-12 hours daily 6 days a week.

If you can't live without modern conveniences you wouldn't like it here; in my apartment there is no over-under combo microwave, range and oven, no garbage disposer, dishwasher or trash compactor. Every day I sweep my floors. Cooking takes much longer on a two-burner propane gas stove – not much bigger than a camping stove – but is a household standard. A washer-dryer combo would be nice but while I wish with one hand I wash with the other, dishes, underwear, you name it. Until recently I had no hot water; I'm lucky – most of my neighbors use only cold water as is the case in most of the country.

If you hate hot things you'd hate it here; they use the word *garam* for both weather and in cooking. Both register in the higher scale of the thermometer! I must say, however, the monsoon has been rather pleasant like a cool crisp *mosambi*, a refreshing beverage made of sweet lime juice.

If you're afraid of bugs, creepy crawlers, and the host of creatures great and small you wouldn't like it here. When I stayed on a farm in Uttar Pradesh there were lots of mosquitoes, flies, big black ants, beetles the size of Mrs. Sees chocolates, frogs, several lizards, two mice and a hornets nest – and, dear Brother – these were all in my

1

bedroom! Here in Bangalore, I'm in the outskirts, we have a couple of full grown black king cobras in our backyard; cows and buffalo in the front—I've been meaning to find out who they belong to?!—and more varieties of tropical birds than you'll find at the San Francisco zoo. (Incidentally, that's where our parents adopted you!) Animal World should come and film here.

If you can't stand suffering, struggling and human strife you wouldn't like it here. India is a developing nation, and although has reached some great plateaus in science, technology, art, and philosophy, all subjects you know nothing about! — it still has a way to go before reaching our *fat cat* Western economic standard. Many foreigners are appalled to see poverty. Even though their religious upbringing teaches them to be kind, compassionate and charitable when the rubber meets the road and they actually confront these conditions they become rude and resentful. The first time a beggar stuck his hand out your *Brotherman* mistook the gesture as a friendly welcome and shook it! Later I stuffed it with coin of the realm.

If you're afraid of challenges that sometimes seem insurmountable you wouldn't like it here; but I find by rising to these challenges it stimulates my intellect and brings out the best in me. (I know you are from the shallow end of the gene pool but even tadpoles can become frogs. You just need to believe in your dream.) I'm always thinking of ways to make a difference. Like a ship cuts through the ocean, I cruise through my day carrying a cargo, always looking ahead towards the port, never behind at my wake.

If you're afraid to learn new things that will greatly improve your life – that's okay; I'll understand. Stay where you are. Where you are is where you belong.

ॐ

Moving the Masses
Building an Infrastructure

Maybe it's the fact that I play Rock 'n Roll, or that my parents allowed me to play with loaded guns as a child, or being a Scorpio—but every once in a while I find myself loosing my cool—I'm talking *borderline ballistic*—when I'm trying to take care of business in Bangalore. It seems like it takes forever to get from Point A to Point B even when it's right around the corner. Have you ever stopped and wondered why?

Infrastructure is a fascinating subject, and of course, the physical foundation societies are built upon. Cities are quite fascinating constructs. Archeologist excavating Mohenjo Dharo, North India, circa 12,000 BC concluded the city had a well developed infrastructure with wide roads, sewers and rain runoff drains. They even found pipes and suspect the early Indians had water plumbed in to three-story high apartment buildings!

The more people you put together the more careful the planning to insure that the massive conglomeration runs smoothly. Probably the biggest problem facing urban development is planning roads, highways and byways, and public transportation systems for moving the masses. When I lived in New York it never took longer than 20-30 minutes to get anywhere in the city using the subway. I was glad when planners finally got the ball rolling in San Francisco. They literally dug up the streets and constructed an enclosed underground tunnel providing Rapid Transit for thousands of daily commuters. It's fast, smooth, clean, quiet, environmentally friendly and relatively inexpensive when compared to cars.

3

Buses are pretty much like they are here—in abundance, running often, and very economical. Because of the extremely high quality of emissions most new buses in America are run on LPG, and the older buses still in service using diesel cannot be *gross polluters*. The law is strictly enforced.

Of course by far the most utilized form of transportation are POV's, private owned vehicles. California has over 30 million—that's one car per person—for every man, woman and child! I won't tell you how many I own. (I'm downsizing.) Studies show 92 percent of the vehicles on the road during the rush hour have only one passenger in them. And though I would love to see all of the citizens of Bangalore blessed with the same sort of freedom of mobility, can you imagine the nightmare traffic problem it would create? Motorcycles and scooters seem to be very practical in terms of fuel and space economy.

In January this year I visited Mexico City. With 21 million people it has the distinction of being the largest city in the world. Mexicans enjoy incomes twice your national average and car sales are booming. Problem—there's no way you're going to get that many local cars on the road, plus all the inbound vehicles from abroad. Solution: Vehicles with license plates ending in the number 3 and 5 cannot drive on public roads on Wednesday, 2 and 4 on Thursday, etc. On any given day of the week 20% of the vehicles are restricted from driving. My number ended in 3 and sure enough, guess who got pulled over by the *policia*? After explaining my ignorance in my best *Espanol* and a friendly handshake—with fifty pesos in it—and I was off the hook!

Highways, freeways and overpasses are imperative to the smooth flow of traffic. Bangalore has the traffic but it doesn't have the roads. Visit New Delhi around the airport and Rastpati Bhavan and see how smoothly things flows with wide, well delineated lanes, traffic signals and dedicated turn lanes. What's holding up the show in Big

B? Pure and simple—management. City and state officials get involved in public works projects and nothing gets done. For 6 months they've been replacing the road in front of my house and have made a muddy mess out of a project that should have taken three weeks. And, the end is nowhere in sight. Why? Government officials are involved. First, someone has stolen the money earmarked for the project — excuse me—misplaced it. Secondly, they are using coolie day laborers with hand shovels. If a paving crew came in with skip loaders, graders, compactors and an asphalt machine the road would be finished. It is a wealthy neighborhood; *vakils* have been called. We suspect nepotism – that the contract to build the road has been awarded to a family member and not a licensed road engineer, and to get rich, the relatives are spending the least amount of money, hiring grunts, hence, terribly delaying the project's completion.

For five years they've been building the overpass on Airport Road near Manipal Hospital! The project manager's fingernails and hair have grown long like a *rishi*. The steelwork on the brand new project is all rusting and the end is nowhere in sight. You can't build an infrastructure like this, people, taking years to complete projects that could be completed in months.

Bangalore is in desperate need of a City Manager with a construction background. Hire experienced pros; have architects draw up plans based on engineering reports and project requirements; have the legal department put together tight contracts; put the contracts out to bid; then sit back and watch how fast things get done. The slowest way to complete a building project is to let the government manage it. Having worked in government construction management I observed government is never motivated to hurry—ever. And, why should it be? The employees receive their fat paychecks regardless whether the work gets done or not. *They have no incentive*. When a decision needs to be made government will take forever because they are bogged down in bureaucracy, having to interface with other agencies and egos, wasting time, leaving behind a huge paper trail. Now, in the real world—the private sector—contractors bid low because they want the work, then accelerate completing the work. When problems occur the project manager together with his associates make rapid informed decisions. Why? Because the quicker the work is done the greater the contractor's profit. Simple economics; standard business practices; a principal that would behoove the nation to adopt in general.

Why be concerned with whether it takes one hour to get to work or ten minutes? Ever since humans climbed down from trees they've been progressively evolving this interconnectedness called *society*. With each new technological advancement things get a little easier for us. As our workload and time demands lessen we find we have more time for *leisure*. And, without leisure there is no art, music, picnics, time for the kids. In the West we work five days a week, eight hours a day and love our 'down time'. *Bharat*, you're such a busy hardworking nation. You need to get from Point A to B and should insist that your city leaders do what they're paid to do—move the society forward. If they can't—get fresh horses! It's that simple. You deserve a breather, kicking back in your e-z chair, and reading a book or some secular article by a daydreaming foreigner.

৵৽

Meter Maids & Radar Traps
Infrastructure Revenue Sources

There is a tribe in Africa whose word for *architecture* is the same as *maintenance*. They have centuries-old buildings and understand that they continually require upkeep. In that tribe each member contributes some labor towards this goal. In our community in Monterey, California—one of the most beautiful coastal communities in America—with citizens like actor Clint Eastwood, Julie Packard of HP Computers—we have a large *Public Works Department*. Public Works keeps the streets clean, changes the light fixtures, paint signs and equipment, insure all the sewers and waste water systems work, keep our roads free from pothole, and maintain all the public common areas. When you visit my town you'll see how clean and well kept everything is.

With such a large workforce of lazy big-belly city workers—there is a constant dialog about *outsourcing* to the private sector—how do the citizens pay for all this? Taxation is the major source of revenue. The Tax Assessors Office sends us assessments based on our property's value at the time of purchase and we make two yearly payments. I pay $3,200 (about Rs. 1.2 lakh) a year in property tax. Of course, my good buddy Clint Eastwood pays ten times more. When you take into consideration the billions of dollars of land in our community—tax revenue adds up.

Every business, regardless of whether you are mowing lawns or manufacturing tiles for the aerospace industry requires you purchase a business license from the city. Thinking of doing a home improvement? Possibly an upstairs room addition? You'll need to purchase a permit from the city based on the value of the improvement. You will hear Americans complain: "Government would tax the air you breathe if they could figure out how to meter it!"—but the revenue earmarked for the city—after paying employees' salaries—is spent primarily on infrastructure. *It's a good thing.*

Another source of revenue comes from parking in the downtown areas. The city owns and operates multistoried parking lots where you pay a couple of bucks per hour to park. Or, they have measured, marked and metered parking spaces on public roads. Cars usually park parallel and motorcycles at an oblique to assure the maximum conservation of space. Each space has a coin-operated meter where we insert coins and the time is digitally displayed. The city hires *meter maids*, special police officers, and as the name denotes, quite often younger women, who ride around on 3-wheelers marking vehicle tires with chalk, returning later to issue *parking violations* if you've exceeded your time limit. When I was a kid I managed to chalk-up $350 in parking tickets in 3 days in New York City—setting some kind of city record!

The City Tax Collectors wring a few more bucks out of our tourists—if you sleep in our town you pay a *hotel tax*. And, all of us who love those great West Coast restaurants have to pay sales tax to eat in them. *There's no free ride.* These combined activities add up to millions of dollars which the City Manager, (after skimming some cream off the top—just kidding, folks!) working within the directives of the Mayor moves the society forward. If the Mayor and City Manager are not effective in accelerating social progress they are booted out at the next election.

The State also contributes to each individual city or township. Retail merchants charge gasoline tax at 7.5% on all non-food items. The biggest sales tax is from automobile and gasoline sales. The State disburses some of this tax revenue back to the cities and towns based upon a formula. The State derives revenues from other sources such as *sin tax*—for those citizens who smoke tobacco products and consume alcohol. And *luxury tax* for people purchasing boats and private airplanes. They've got you by the short hairs if you happen to be a smoking jet setter! Personal *income tax* is the pie's biggest slice.

Believe it or not *law enforcement* also rakes in a considerable chunk of change. In California law enforcement has become high tech and automated. Be careful driving in the San Francisco Bay Area. I received an automatically generated notice in the mail demanding payment for a company truck an employee had driven through an automatic tollgate on the Golden Gate Bridge. A camera had caught the violation. *Doppler cameras* mounted on freeway overpasses monitor speed and will automatically ticket any speeding violators. It's getting to the point where you can't get away with anything!

Regardless of how you cut the cake the bottom line is it takes a lot of money to efficiently run a city. The more money, the more services for the citizens. Americans are spoiled. Let's face it, we like our communities safe, clean and easy to get around in. A good working government, whose employees are well paid and have a sense of community pride and high moral standard are pivotal tools. A good mayor with a fat budget can literally make miracles happen. The mayor of Chicago, John Daily, was so good at running the city they kept him in office for twenty years. And when you visit Chicago your head will spin. It is a garden of architectural wonder, with breathtaking buildings, well laid out park-like neighborhoods, intelligently planned, efficiently managed. When you visit a place like Chicago or San Francisco or Seattle you go away impressed with what modern humans have been able to accomplish in societal organization. Bangalore also has that showcase potential. You've already got a great start with many beautiful buildings, like the Leela

Palace Hotel and the Manipal Center commercial complex. Take a drive through Jayanagar or Koramangala or around Cubbon Park. There is a lot of beauty here. But, it takes money and good management to run a city. Right now you need a team of workhorses to fast track the infrastructure. But, I'm sorry to say, I just don't see it happening. *Look around you.* New buildings and communities are mushrooming everywhere. But, where are the roads? the freeways? the overpasses? the mass transit? the public works? the law enforcement? the emergency services? If your municipal government doesn't have a vision of tomorrow which is producing results today, they are working against you—not for you. What this city needs is not politicians who talk a good game plan—but veteran managers with proven track records in getting the job done based on a solid game plan. Bangalore—the future is knocking. Open the door and welcome it in.

Pissing in Public
Answering Mother Nature's Call

What do street dogs and Bangalore gents have in common? Give up? Neither are the slightest bit concerned about pissing wherever and whenever they please—pissing on walls, sidewalks, streets, high traffic areas—some piss on trees, lawns and bushes—I'm talking about the guys, not the dogs. I always love the story of the Queen of England's visit; while being escorted through Bangalore by Prime Minister Indira Gandhi, appalled, the Queen Elizabeth, pointed and asked, *"What are those men doing?"* and kindhearted Ms.Gandhi replied, "Easing themselves, dear." Of course, the English have been using flush toilets since 1514, the first being owned by none other than the Grand Dame herself. In the late 1880's a guy by the name of William Crapper invented the standard gravity system that we use today, and, as we all know *crap* is synonymous with some unpleasant business we all need to tend to on a regular basis.

For a long time I wondered, "Do their parents teach them this behavior or do they learn it from their pets?" Then I got a break. Downtown the other day I saw a guy in a business suit striding along the sidewalk, briefcase in hand. Suddenly he made a beeline for a tree, unhostered his pisser and took a whiz—at that very moment several buses of school children happened by. *Men are teaching the behavior to future generations.* (Okay. Perhaps they acquire the finesse by studying their pooches!)

In the West not only is pissing in public considered uncivilized—it's against the law. To expose your genitals in public—even though some guys think it's a great way to meet girls—is called *indecent exposure*. And, is going to cost you! Also, 'easing yourself' is a criminal offense that violates the *public health code*. Both carry a Rs 10,500 fine and/or one year in jail for your first offense. Although I've never met anybody who actually served jail time I have met guys who *got caught with their pants down* and had to pay the fine. As your relationship with the West increases so will the influx of visiting foreigners. Boys, it's time to clean up your act.

You will be pleased to learn that if you are amongst those men who cannot hold their pee-pee from the time they leave the house until they get to the office, *you're gonna love me*. I have several personal relief design patents and am considering having a major Indian manufacturer start production as soon as I can work out the marketing. You can choose from two designs in a variety of colors. *Bala Bladder* is a flatten balloon reservoir with a small check valve that assures fluid flow in one direction only. For the effective operation of this devise it is imperative that you have the valve in the right direction or for certain you'll piss your pants. Sorry ladies, this product is only available for men. However, may I suggest, *Port-A-Potty*, an ingenious device with a *gender attachment* that adapts to any human fluid delivery system and drains into a liner easily concealed beneath a business suit or sari. Piss anywhere, piss anytime! We're working on a model called the *Duryodan* which can be inserted rectally to provide freedom of the bowels too. I see a big market especially with visiting foreigners who usually experience *Duryodan's Revenge* during their first month or two in India!

With over a billion liters of urine being passed daily—who says there's a water shortage in India? If one of your Tech-nicks could invent a high-speed purification system—like NASA uses for the astronauts—Bangalore City could recycle the pee and pipe back into the tap water system—it couldn't taste any worst than it already does! (One astronaut recently commented: *"All this time I thought we were drinking Tang orange juice!"*)

Public health is a social problem that requires a government solution. In California it is very easy to find a public *rest room,* as they are politely called. By law, every commercial building has one, every gas station, restaurant, pubic park or area designated for recreation or pubic assembly. During a big event, or in locations where plumbing and sewage are not available, the government provides and maintains plastic toilet units – usually providing more toilets for ladies than gents – not that it takes longer to do their business, but their clothing takes more time to navigate. Cheap, transportable, convenient. In downtown San Francisco you'll find spiffy looking kiosks imported from France. As an employer I am required by law to provide a toilet if I have more than 3 workers. If you're taking a long road trip and need to answer the call of Nature *rest areas* are conveniently located along the highways where you can stop, stretch, dispose of your trash, purchase refreshments, and do your business. Why—you'll even find areas designated for pets. (Occasionally, we get a guy visiting from Bangalore who finds the temptation just too irresistible!) Toilets are everywhere. Hey—it's no big deal. If you need to go—you need to go. It seems to me that your city planners should *get off the pot* and do something about the problem, rather than allowing the city to become one big stinking disgusting toilet. They cry, *"There's nowhere to put them."* Well, find room!—even if it means putting them underground. Do it! and like our *Governator*, Arnold Schawartznegger tells Congress, "DO IT NOW!" If the city planners can't find workable solutions to improve the basic condition of their own city—flush them. It's time for some fresh horses—know what I mean, Jellybean?!? *Bharat,* if you can put a satellite in outer space, you surly can put public toilets in trafficked areas.

You know— the more I think about it the better Port-A-Potty sounds. Or, at least, adult-size diapers! We could call them *Bala Bibs* and make a ton of money. What do you think?

13

Cowboys in Bangalore
Urban Animal Control Officers

I was having an emergency and needed to get my laptop to the PC doctor ASAP. Putting the spurs to my auto driver we flew down Mahatma Gandhi Road—MG for those who know it well—out toward Tech Park—when suddenly my cab came to a screeching halt. Horns honking, drivers shaking their fist, traffic at a standstill. *There must be an accident up ahead*, I thought. *Just my luck*. I decided to investigate and climbed up on the roof of the rickshaw—those Bajaj's are made pretty well—and, as my driver pleaded with me to come down, I spied the source of our delay. A couple of cows had decided to take a *siesta* in the middle of the road!

Since coming to India I've seen pigs, goats, horses, chickens, dogs, donkeys and a few wild looking *sadhus*, and I'm only talking on my own street! You will find wild livestock in every corner of town. When I read the brochures on coming to India there was some mention about *holy cows* roaming freely and that they were worshipped. Believe me folks, the cows laying in the middle of the city's major traffic artery were anything but being worshipped. Cows are beautiful creatures. I waft back in time, hearing the *kankanas* of Gopala as he danced ahead of the herd merrily *muraling* in the sylvan hills of Brindavan. Then I snap back to Twenty-first Century reality. Cows and all domestic livestock belong on farms in rural communities—not in a metropolis. Dogs are man's best friend. In Bangalore there are hundreds of feral dogs that could sure use a friend. Get a grip, City Planners. Who's in charge here—the simians or the sapiens?

The city's already a mess with humans using every wall, bush and tree for a toilet. (See: Pissing In Public.) It's bad enough as is without having to dodge cow pies and donkey doo! The idea of an outdoor interactive zoo has it's appeal—*on another planet.* Or, perhaps you can introduce the city to potential tourists as a theme park. Dad will bring the whole family and after making a few pivotal software deals he can take the kids for a ride around town to see the menagerie. What's wrong with this picture?

I'll share something with you. My wife grew up never having a pet so one day we went to the Animal Shelter, where they house mostly dogs and cats – but a few more exotic pets like rattlesnakes and tarantula spiders owners have abandoned—(a little American eccentricity!)—and adopted a feisty dog my wife named *Tesa*, after a river in her native country. One day I came home from work and found the gate to the yard flung open and our pet pooch gone. I felt a sense of relief—do you have any idea how much responsibility pet ownership is? At the same time a sense of grief knowing how much my wife loved Tesa. As I began preparing a gourmet dinner hoping it would help offset her upset—the telephone rang. It was a call from the *animal control officers.* They had good news—depending on whose viewpoint—and bad news. The good news was they had Tesa safely in their possession. The bad news was I needed to come pick her up and bring $125 (Rs 5,250!) – $45 for breaking the city leash law that requires all domestic animals be 'under the control of their owner at all times', $45 for violating the city animal license law that requires 'all domestic animals to be issued and wear an identification notice', and the $35 impound fee which helps to defray the government's operational costs. *They really sock it to you!*

When I got to the shelter, and after paying the fine, I asked the *animal control officer* how in the world did they ever identify the dog and get our unlisted telephone number. **NOW HEAR THIS**: at the time we adopted the dog they inserted a tiny inexpensive chip the size of a grain of rice painlessly under the skin of her ear. All they had to do was to scan the ear. With the bar code they were able to trace the dog's history. All in a few minutes. Okay—so it cost me an arm and a leg to get my wife's dog back. But, it was worth it. You husbands can relate. Believe me—the following day I was up early and out in the backyard fixing the gate and any and every escape route that hound could find! It was an expensive lesson. But, one worth noting by your City Planners. You do not find stray animals very often in California.

Developing or copying this technology would be a piece of cake for the Whiz Kids over on Tech Road. And, *Bharat*, lets think 'improving society' not 'fattening my wallet' (though you're welcomed to try). It is our duty as custodians of the planet to look after the welfare of all the animals and particularly those we interact with. A humane society is one that understands the meaning of *loka samasta sukino bavantu.* (Need an interpreter?) So, here's the deal: All pet owners are required to license their animals—you figure out a low cost. Each pet gets an ear tag. Livestock owners have a different problem because they can't put their cows, goats and horses in the backseat of a Bajaj—even though we've seen them try! So, their registration cost is a bit higher because the *animal control officers* (so many per district) will have to drive their vehicles, which serve the dual purpose of picking up strays or injured animals, to the cow and do the implant on site. (It's a little staple gun that shoots a biocompatible bar code. Painless, fast, cheap.) When an animal officer finds a cow in the middle of the road, first they will quickly get it to the side so that *my auto* can go, scan the ear, use their mobile phone to call headquarters who in turn will contact the owner. If the owner can't be contacted, or there is no implant, a livestock cart will be dispatched, pick up the cow and take it to an impound. The owner will have 7 days to come pay their fines (hefty ones) or loose the animal. What to do with a corral full of cows? *You city boys know nothing.* Ask your rural brothers! Where do you think ice cream comes from—donkeys?! And, keep in mind, there are still millions of people importing beef. The Japanese pay the highest prices. *Bharat,* you can do this; it just takes a civic mind—you may even find a few at City Hall—and a little hard work. Easy peasy!

Do you know how much time and human productivity is lost everyday because of domestic livestock related incidents? *If you do please let me know.* But, all of us have experienced this—and, on numerous occasions. I am trying to dialog with City Planners—they still won't pick up the phone—to see about bringing a few of my cowboy friends over from the States. I know some guys in Wyoming and Montana that would have a regular rodeo right in downtown Bangalore! Now wouldn't that be a sight.

Beasts of Burden
An Anarchronism on the Hoof

A farmer from the middle part of the United States raised several cows from calves. He was extremely fond of them and always sang to them as he led them to pasture. One day, after being pastured, the cows became startled and the man looked up just in time to see a raging bull rushing straight towards him. Somehow the gate separating the two areas had opened. There was nowhere to run; nowhere to hide. The bull barreled into the man goring him in the chest; the impact sent him flying through the air and crash landing. Momentarily, the bull stopped. Then, spotting the victim, the bull started pawing the ground preparing for another attack. But, before the charge the cows formed a protective ring around the man. Enraged, the bull attacked the cows killing two before ranch hands saw what was going on and were able to distract and lure the bull back into it's own yard. Of all the stories I've ever heard about the love bond that can form between man and animal, this is special.

Human history has been forged with *brute strength*. A symbiosis has evolved between man and domestic livestock. While my ancestors were trying to stay warm in caves in Europe yours were fighting epic battles with horse mounted Calvary and elephants. The ruler with the most muscle usually swayed the balance of power. Even today when man has all the horsepower he requires under the hood of his Tata or Leyland Ashok, animals are still an essential part of suburban and rural India. In the metropolitan they are nothing but a nuisance. (See: Cowboys In Bangalore.) Besides, how happy can a cow or bullock be in a concrete pasture? Sometimes I ask myself the same question?!?

Even though statistics are not readily available, as with licensed vehicles, the number of oxen and carts must be substantial and into the lakhs in Karnataka alone. We see them daily engaged in all manner of manual labor; delivering building materials to job sites, hauling loads of produce and general merchandise, pulling carts heaped with garbage—just look out your window. But, to be the physical engines of man's commercial conveyances is not an animal's natural inclination. It is a role man has assigned the creature. The bullock and cows have their own *dharma* that would do us well to study. For instance, a cow will not eat meat—ever. If an animal has been killed in the field and the grass is wet with its blood the cow will not eat the grass—even if it's hungry. It adheres strictly to the dictates of instinct and follows Nature's prompting without deviation. A wise man could learn much from his *second mother*.

Chances are if you own and work with dray animals you will not be reading this passage of thought. But if by chance you know someone who does, please remind them to thank the animals for their service every time they are harnessed to the yoke of our endeavors. Their dream is of green pastures and peaceful herds. Alone, they care for themselves. But, they are in your charge and depend on you for their sustenance and support. If you can't take care of your animals in a humane manner you have no business owning them. On behalf of the beasts of burden who cannot articulate their demands below are a few simple courtesy.

- It is your duty to provide them with good drinking water often throughout the day.
- It is your duty to feed them. How many of you have seen ribs showing like an old washboard? These animals are worked hard and not fed enough. Their owner is starving them. I would refuse to do business with any vendor whose animal was in such a condition—and report them to the authorities for *animal cruelty*.

- When possible provide shade for them if they have much standby time; and see that they have days of rest—no creature, including man, is meant to work like a machine.
- Be gentle when asking them to perform a task—if they hesitate there may be a reason. I saw a young man furiously whipping the rear haunches of a poor bullock. Obviously he was used to traveling at high speeds on a motorcycle. He didn't like it when I took the whip from his hand and gave him a few hard strokes across his back! He started crying for his *first mother*!
- Carry a little salt or sugar with you for them to lick—you will see they respond like the man who sang to his cows—with love.

The United States has many laws protecting animals, and they are strictly enforced. It would serve you well, *Bharat*, to also protect this silent workforce who can't protect themselves. If I haven't mentioned before, I'm a double Scorpio and very psychic. While trying to collect data for this article I met a guy who owned a few farm animals. When he heard I was psychic, he asked me to look at his chickens who had stopped laying eggs. I put my hand on one bird's tiny head then said to the guy, "There's a whole in their coup and a snake keeps coming in and scaring them. That's why they're not laying eggs." We went to the coup and sure enough, in one corner found a hole in the board. He thanked me and asked if I could look at his cow who had stopped giving milk. I put my hand on her head for a moment then said to the *zamindar*, "She says she's very old and you've been milking her for years. She's just plain tired and won't give anymore." Then I spied a couple of bullocks with ribs sticking out and flies buzzing around festering sores.. "I'm writing a paper on Beasts of Burden. Do you mind it I talk to them?" I asked. The *zamindar* quickly replied, "You don't want to talk to them—*they're lairs!*"

The Brahma bull oxen is part of this country's national history. Even as we race toward the future and the day when animal power will be replaced with kinetic energy devices I hope you will always find a special place to honor the bullock. Have you ever seen the cattlemen of neighboring Andra Pradesh at their annual drives? It's a sight to behold—a convergence of hundreds of magnificent animals with perfect horns and humps, beige and dun colors with the most intelligent eyes. So impressed was I with India's cattle-culture that friends turned Bangalore upside down trying to locate a pair of the decorative silver horn-tips and brass bell-rings that jingle with each lumbering stride. I keep them on my desk. If by chance when Tata phases out bullocks with 4-cylinder pickup trucks and you find there is an overpopulation of 'hoofers' I'd love to adopt a herd, but don't know where to pasture them. Hmmm...I wonder if SFO would rent me that little plot of grass on the shoulder of the main runway?!

Building in Bangalore
Protecting Your Investment

A ruckus outside caught my attention and seeing my neighbor Asha about to clean a contractor's clock I threw on a *lunghi* and dashed to the ground floor. Like a referee in a boxing match I stepped in between the two prize fighters and nudged them apart—it wasn't easy as Asha had a vice grip stranglehold on the man's throat. With some doing the shouting match softened to a tense standoff.

"What's the problem?" I opened the intermediation.

"He's said he'd dig a trench 10 feet long by 2 feet wide and has only dug 6 feet of it and wants me to pay him Rs.4,000! Besides that, the trench is only 22 inches wide," the hardworking account manager pleaded, omitting some details.

The contractor turned his drooping eyes to me, trembling his upturned palms as if supplicating Allah, and explained, "While we were digging we ran into a rock. We're entitled to get paid for the work we've done so far."

"But, he should have finished the work first," she protested, shaking a fist at him.

I peeked in the excavated trench. A rock was an understatement; a stone carver would have liked to have gotten a chisel on this Ganapati-size baby. "Generally, a contractor is not responsible for removing underground obstacles," I explained. "He had no way of knowing it was there before starting to dig. So, you will have to be responsible for hiring a crew to remove the rock to allow the plumber to run his pipe." This news silenced her a little. The contractor took advantage of the pause.

"And, I need to get paid for the work I've done to date. Now!" he demanded.

"Usually, on small jobs, we give an advance—either 10% or $1,000—*which ever is less*. And pay the balance in full when the job is finished. What does your contract say?" I asked. Her rapid eye movement and fidgeting was body language loud and clear.

"*I don't have a contract*," Asha said.

"Lady, I want my money!" the man smacked the back of one hand against the open palm of the other. And, the cat and dog were at it again, him threatening to go to the authorities, she threatening to shoot off his legs! India gals are pretty tough when they're riled up.

As discussed in Legal Weapons, always get it in writing. How much, how many, what quality, and when is what going to be done. The world's first written language appeared—not in Nepal or Nairobi—but here. So use it! When a contract is not written, and all you have are 'he-said-she-said' all is not lost. If there are witnesses willing to testify (I've heard they can be purchased cheaply) they can support a claim. Also, *intent* speaks volumes. In this case the contractor's intent was evident—he had already completed 60% of the work. Was he responsible for the rock? No. Should he be entitled to collect any money before the rock was removed? Perhaps—because of a point of the law known as *reasonable reliance*. In good faith he put a crew to work on her job and had reasonable expectations things would go smoothly. *Do they ever in construction?* Does he deserve to collect 60% for completing that percentage of the job? No. Asha's agreement is to pay Rs.10,000 for 10 feet of trenching. Her most generous offer could have been to pay him 50% and retained 10% to make sure he'd come back. Usually legal clauses like retainers are found in more complicated contracts such as for a house or commercial building. Small home improvement contracts are the most common—we're having a new fence installed, the house painted, a room addition, or, as in Asha's case, a new water line plumbed. You will avoid a lot of problems by getting it in writing. And, when you encounter some difficulty it is best to *mediate a solution*. Remember, in a negotiation, each person has to win—it can't be all one-sided.

I am not familiar with licensing laws in India, but in the United States if a tradesperson, man or woman, gives you a fixed bid to do work on your home for more than $500, which includes both labor and material, they must be *licensed by the State*. The requirements for actual licensing are stringent; you must know and demonstrate by a *government examination* your proficiency in not only the trade of your specialization but also the labor laws, fair business practices and procedures. A licensed contractor has to prove *financial solvency* and post a *performance bond*. Should he fail to perform his obligations you are entitled to go after the bond. Once, a slick contractor from L.A. thought he'd get over on me. By using his license number, which is required to appear on all a contractor's logos, business cards, etc, I was able to track his bonding company and collect my money. Likewise, a licensed contractor has a direct relationship with the property and can file a *mechanic's lien* to insure his payment. Without a license a court will not hear his case and may even issue a fine against him if it is determined he has broken the law. With building booming in Bangalore it seems imperative to have a good legal licensing system, weeding out the fakes and phonies who are only interested in a fast buck from the skilled tradesmen and women who are building your country.

And in closing, a question for my non-Indian readers: Can a foreigner traveling in India on a tourist visa purchase real estate? Answer: Absolutely not. It is against the law. To legally purchase land you must have permanent residency status and follow stringent requirements. I have met several foreigners lured by low prices take the bait only to find out later they'd been swindled by unscrupulous businessmen. I know of one flat that was sold three times in five years to unwary tourists! Tourists can enter into a 99 year lease. However, before entering into any financial investment in India you should consult a good attorney. I did and narrowly escaped becoming a statistic – the fourth owner of the flat that was too good to be true.

Legal Weapons
A Well Written Construction Contract

Rajendran works hard for his money. Following his father from a small village in Tamil Nadu, he settled in Whitefield. His first job washing taxi cabs evolved into driving them. After years of tucking away a few rupees every payday Rajendran scraped together enough money to purchase his first taxi. By working long hours, carefully budgeting and making personal sacrifices Rajendran finally had a nest egg and purchased a piece of land—a place he could call his own. With his good credit the bank loaned him 2 lakh rupees and he hired Mr. Rao, a local contractor who was wealthy and politically connected. Meeting over a cup of chai, the contractor created a dream house and the taxi driver could picture it clearly in his mind's eye. They shook hands to seal the deal and Rajendran gave Mr. Rao 2 lakhs rupees excited about his single most important purchase—a home. But, the dream house Mr. Rao created with words never took shape with concrete. Rajendran tried pressuring Rao but to no avail. Suddenly Rao developed amnesia and couldn't remember having any dealings with Rajendran. When asked to produce a written contract the semi-literate villager was unable to. Rajendran is still driving his taxi, scrimping to repay the bank loan. In another five years, when it's paid off, he will start building his dream house again. Hopefully, next time he will have a well written construction contract.

Before we examine a contract let's review the players. An *architect* designs a building based on the homeowner's requirements. Sometimes they work closely together, sometimes loosely. Some general building contractors offer design services as part of the package. Ask your builder if he also does design. If yes, ask to see drawings of some projects. A *structural engineer* checks the drawings for physical integrity and certifies that the engineering calculations are correct. If the building falls down, we usually find it's the engineer's fault rather than the builder's. A *general building contractor* coordinates all of the *subcontractors*—the roofers, tile setters, painters, etc. Often the general contractor has a crew and is involved in some aspect of the project, e.g., carpentry, wood framing, and concrete. They create and follow schedules, arrange inspections with building officials, monitor cash flow—periodically submitting invoices to the owner for payment, then dispersing the funds to the subcontractors. They stay with the project from start to finish.

In my country the contracting profession is strictly regulated by laws that go back to humanity's first written laws—the Codex of Hammurabi—laws about construction. A good contract protects the homeowner by specifying the scope of work, the quality, price and payment method, the project's commencement and completion, and the consequences if the conditions of the contract are not kept. The first thing you want in your contract after the *names* of both parties is the *site location*. It can be a plot number or a physical description of the property.

<u>Scope of work</u> can be simple or very vague. Example: Once I attended an arbitration representing a US federal government project that specified the *contractor should install a new air conditioning system*. Great! It didn't address any details of quality, capacity, who would pay for design costs, site conditions, etc. The government wound up paying the contractor an additional $100,000! A scope can be quite specific listing the most minute details, such as, fixture brand names and models, tile patterns and grout spacing, paint colors, etc. Regardless of whether your scope of work is simple or complex it should specify that *the work performed is of standard workmanship and in compliance with local and national building codes*. And, you

always want to tie the finished work with the building plan. This gives you legal recourse should the builder not use professionals or deviate from the written drawings.

Payment clause. Your home is your single largest investment. Most of us must take a bank loan. A loan officer can be helpful in setting up a construction account that earns interest on the money while it's still in savings. Your contract should specify how much money and how the contractor will be paid—in a lump sum or as the work progresses? I prefer *progress payments.* On large projects I also ask my contractors to provide me with a *schedule of values* which lists all of the construction phases—site prep, excavation, plumbing, electrical, etc.—and gives each a cost value as well as a percentage value. For example, say your home costs $100,000 total; installing doors and windows costs $10,000 and equals 10% of the total cost. Our contractor submits his monthly invoice and, in addition to all the other subcontractors who have worked on the project, we see the windows and doors are only 50% complete. We would pay $5,000 for that billing cycle. Like many owners I like a contract clause that allows me to retain 10% of the contractor's money for 30 days after his final building inspection and filing a *notice of completion*—a legal instrument that allows you to take occupancy of the new house. The retainer gives me time to make sure everything is working properly—toilets flushing, door bells ringing, pipes not singing, etc. You'd be surprised how fast a contractor will return your phone call when you are holding his money. Under no circumstance should you pay more than 10%, *down payment*, in advance. It's against the law for the contractor to demand more.

Commencement & completion. In addition to rent, you are also paying the bank interest on the money you've borrowed. When you hire a contractor you need him to commit to a start and completion date. If he's too busy to make a commitment find someone who isn't. State in writing what *punitive damages* he will pay you in the event he fails to start and finish the project on time. I've seen contracts that compound the interest daily. On large projects these penalties can be brutal. In all fairness there are certain conditions that humans have no control over—the biggest being the weather. Some flexibility may be required. Spell it out in writing.

Cancellation right. A contract is a legally binding document. A standard contract gives you the right to cancel the contract within 72 hours with signed written notice.

Your new home should be a dream-come-true not an ongoing nightmare.

[Editor's note: Construction laws in India may vary from laws in America. Please consult your attorney prior to signing a construction contract.]

My Little Cash Cow
Fundamentals of Small Business

[Editor's note: The original draft of this little book excluded this article. But, given the urgency of fast forwarding India's economic development, it is included hoping a few readers may literally profit.]

True or false—corporations comprise the biggest piece of the pie called the *Gross National Product? (GNP)* If you answered 'true' you're absolutely wrong! Small business does. Do you want to know statistically how big that slices is? I'll tell you...

Since I was old enough to ride a bike and had an interest in my personal economy—I had a business. My first, a newspaper route that netted about Rs.1,650 a month. For a ten-year old kid not a bad chunk of change. At fifteen, my second—a live bait business I purchased from a military man moving to Vietnam. It included a small boat, several shrimp traps, and a 55-gallon holding tank. The only set back was the location of my 'raw materials'—deep in the jungle of Panama with the risk of snake bite, leopard attack or running into Durian tribals—human head hunters. After a stint in the army, which qualified me for educational benefits, I choose facilities maintenance. But, after a few years bouncing around employers I decided it was time to hang out my own shingle and started my first adult business providing independent maintenance service. The ride was rough and though I had more than enough customers from one marketing source I found that I lacked education in management. After several years the house of cards collapsed. Caught in the fast moving current of Western economy I grabbed on to employment with the Federal Government, which proved to be a good choice. Starting on the ground floor within a few years I climbed the ladder enough where I was pulling down a good salary, had an office, secretary, and company car. The real perks were the education the government provided, paying for my college tuition in construction management. In addition, I studied Small Business. With a steady day job I decided I'd take another crack at it.

Business plans: The elements of a small business can be summarized into about five major components. The first step is to create a *business plan* with an opening paragraph that clearly defines what you'd ultimately like to accomplish. The plan can include an assessment of the competition, what materials or equipment is required, what are the initial startup costs and projected profits, and how you intend to gradually build the business until achieving your goal. A *marketing plan* is usually included as a separate section of the business plan. It spells out how you plan to sell your goods or services. I decided to provide construction site clean-up and, after considering the competition, opted for displayed advertising in the telephone directory. Another good choice.

Bank loans: I needed a couple of good trucks, some specialty hydraulic equipment and a page of miscellaneous items. Based on my steady income and good business plan the bank loaned me $20,000 and set up a payment schedule over a five year period. The loan was repaid within two years, which boosted my credit scores qualifying me for even greater loan amounts. Establishing good credit is essential for growth.

Business license: You need to know the requirement in your community. In ours a business license was required. I also discovered there were specialty licenses for different types of material handling, such as asbestos. I jumped through the hoops. The greater your credentialing the more *scoring opportunities*. Soon I had major accounts including the federal and state governments using our service.

Insurance: Things might be a little different in India, but in the West we pay through the nose for insurance. Because of fraudulent insurance claims, the cost of *worker's compensation* is astronomical— in some trades 50% of an employee's wage! The law requires we carry this insurance if we employ people. So, I had no choice. But, even though it was expensive it opened doors that would have otherwise remained closed. I also needed *general liability,* in case my company did any damage to our customers' property. And, I also had to carry *commercial auto* for the company trucks. In the beginning I would cringe to see how much insurance ate up the profits. But, by being insured, the company was completely legit and could run with the Big Dogs.

Accounting & administrative: What I'm telling you is important— if you don't like paperwork a small business might not be a good choice for you. I had good phone skills and a great phone system – if I was out of the office the calls would forward to a mobile phone and if no one was available the call would rollover into a mailbox that would activate a pager. If you're paying for classified advertising never want to miss a call. We kept our appointments and were on top of our billing. And, as a consequence *our business made a ton of money*— a figure of speech. I liked to sell the work, generate the invoices, and—the best part—go to the bank! I subcontracted our *payroll* and let a *chartered accountant* keep us square with government taxs— both federal and state.

After years of trying I had put together the right combination and owned a *little cash cow.* Within a few years I purchased my first piece of real estate—and, on the West Coast property values are like they are in downtown Bangalore – *bahut mahaga hai!* However, a word to the wise—a small business is not the best option for everyone.

They seem to work well for extremely independent people and those who are good at self-motivating. When I was leaving my good paying government job to take care of my little cash cow, my supervisor confided that he'd always dreamed of owning his own business but was afraid of both failure *and* success. He had a family, so taking the risk was understandable. But, *fear of success?* I didn't get it. Then he explained that he was afraid that if there was money in the bank he might not be motivated to get up in the morning and put in a full day. I smiled at him and affectionately shook his hand. Although he was a loving man, he didn't have my philosophy. He hadn't been to India to study the *Vedanta*. His vocabulary missed the word *dharma*. We don't work because we have to—*we work because it is our duty*. In the great philosophical writing of Vedavyasa who supposedly wrote down the words of Lord Krishna's dialog with the great king-warrior Arjuna Pandava, the Lord told the king, "Do your duty and surrender the fruits unto me". And, you will see, that when you live your life accordingly, your work becomes divine. Do we stop working just because we've attained some socio-economic plateau? Of course not— we find other projects. (See: Community Service). Life is short— why shorten it further by becoming a lazy good for nothing millionaire?!?

Now—if you said small business accounts for 70% of the GNP you're absolutely correct. It's the backbone of free enterprise.

Snooze You Loose
The Cost of Lost Productivity

Mr. Nagaraj, the owner of a playground manufacturing company had scheduled a 2:00 o'clock appointment to give us a bid on furbishing a school with about Rs 100,000 worth of new stationary toys. I had coordinated the primary players, the chief executive officer of the school and the property owner who had agreed to the improvements. Two o'clock came and went. No Mr. Nagaraj. Embarrassed at his tardiness, I apologized to the principals and called him on his cell phone. "I'm still in Bangalore—do you think we can make it at 4:30?" Quickly, I tabulated the collective hours we would have to wait and told him: "If you loose your health or wealth a doctor and charted accountant can help recover them. However, if you loose a minute of time—not even God can get it back for you!"

Nagaraj's failure to live up to his commitment reflects a national pattern I have observed consistently. If I was a jerk—which I can be—I would have had my attorney draft a demand for payment citing *Reasonable Reliance* as the legal grounds. Three professional people had modified our schedules, blocked out the time, expended money and energy based on his word that he would meet us. The fact he owned a reputable company we felt we could *reasonably rely* on his verbal commitment. Had his plans changed the curtsey of a phone call could have preserved the integrity of our business relationship, at the same time saved the loss of one lakh of business for his company. By law, a judge would award us *actual damages*—the three of us could have submitted and received payment for a half day of work at our normal compensation. Of course—Nagaraj would pass bricks if he had to pay mine!

The water delivery didn't bring water the day he said he would; the driver for my doctor's appointment didn't show up, making me very late, besides casting me in a bad light. The plumber didn't show yesterday and didn't call. The same with the *butcher, baker & candlestick maker!* So, often have Indian citizens said they would do something at a specific time on a specific day and failed to perform that I've developed a distrust and take whatever they say with a grain of salt – and sometimes a shot of Tequilla! After so many repeated experiences even a slow learner will start to get the picture. Indian people, often, fail to meet their commitments. Their credibility is ruined. And, my friends, in this fast paced world of expanding economy—*credibility* is a virtue akin to *transparency*. No one wants to interact with a person who can't keep their word. In the West time is money and no one likes to waste either.

I've been in many countries that stop working during the day and take naps—like little children in nursery school. Have you had this experience: you're in the middle of a project—whatever it is— you need certain components to complete it and take a trip to the commercial center only to find the *specialty shop closed.* After awhile you learn their schedule and modify your own. It's inconvenient and not only looses potential income for the shopkeeper but also wastes your time and productivity. In California, we have *superstores* that open early and close late. A couple I do business with are *Office Depot* where you can purchased all items related to home, school or the office environment from pencil lead refills to the most modern PC's with in-store technical support. Why, they even stock a large selection of office furniture, desks, credenzas, bookcases, files cabinets in an assortment of woods—which they deliver and assemble. Another *depot* is the *Home Depot*, who is a large employer in Bangalore and Hyderabad for outsource calls related to account inquiries. The *Home Depot* is a 120,000 square foot complex that stocks everything from modern kitchens and bathrooms, to landscape and gardening. It is a favorite with both builders and homeowners. Hours: 6:30 am – 10:00 pm, everyday.

The *plighted word* was sacred to Lord Rama—so much so that he was willing to sacrifice his family, his wife, his kingdom and his own personal comfort to uphold words his father had promised Rama's stepmother. This country has a history of great kings and Godmen upholding the principals of *dharma* as their highest duty. Your ancestors would disown you if they saw how careless you are with time and commitments. Where and when did this bad habit begin and what can be done to correct it?

Scheduling: In construction management we use several different organizational systems to plan, implement and track activity. Your day is a micro construction project, full of activity that helps float your boat and steer it toward the future. First project of the day— build that perfect cup of coffee. I'm not suggesting you use a complex flow chart that show diagrammatically each component of your day— brush teeth at 6:34am; comb hair at 6:38; eat breakfast at 6:42; kiss wife goodbye at 7:05—but a few simple *home-admin* tools can help smooth out the wrinkles.

I prefer a *wall mount calendar* over a desktop calendar because you can see the month at a glance. I also use a large *30-day organizer* wall mounted in my office with erasable color markers. With a big 2' x 3' board there is never any doubt about what work is scheduled for the day. One year my wife gave me a *palm PC*, which electronically allowed me the freedom to create a schedule. I found it too time consuming and that you had to constantly be laboriously entering data, then checking. After playing with it a while I gave the high-tec toy to a foreign exchange student!

Fudge Factor: Never schedule specific times—in India. Given your horrible infrastructure and gridlock traffic, and God forbid –

encounters with domestic livestock! – how can anyone who isn't psychic predict when they will arrive at Point B when they're still trying to get out of the driveway at Point A? A 15 to 30 minute spread seems reasonable.

Common Courtsey: And, for heaven's sake, if you're running late or are not going to be able to make your appointment call the other person and explain the situation. A phone call is not only common courtsey it is a mark of professionalism. If you hang me up once—I may forgive you. Twice—I'll 'circular file' your business card! I don't have time for people who like to waste mine.

⤫⤬

Don't Be A Litterbug
Trashing a Nation

We were on our way to Joshimath, high in the mountains of Uttaranchal when the driver of the lead vehicle of our four-car caravan pulled to the side of the road. It was a lovely little spot with a commanding view of unnamed Himalayan peaks, forested stands, hillside terraces, and streams spilling into a meandering river—the beginning of the Holy Ganges—a mist cooled the valley far below. We stood transfixed momentarily by the magnetic splendor, then one of the employees cracked out lunch and distributed parcels. Why does food taste so much better in spots of great natural beauty? Suddenly, to my astonishment our host, a retired scientist, and his entire entourage began throwing their trash on the ground, defiling this sacred spot as if it were nothing! I couldn't believe my eyes. Vehemently I protested. "*India is a beautiful country. Don't be a litterbug.*" But, when they continued to trash the land I became irate and started picking up their garbage. Then I threatened to throw them over the side of the cliff if they didn't stop immediately—at six foot tall and 86 kgs — *I'm your guy.* I only had to throw one of them over—a little chap—a chartered account or something like that—to convince them I meant business!

Bharat, kya bat hai? Why are you trashing yourself like this? It hurts you in many ways. As a friend I'd like to share a few observations and help instill you with a little more pride about your beautiful country. I'll suggest some things that you can do personally, and that government can do to help keep it clean. Did you know if you throw an apple core or banana peel on the ground it takes about a week for the moisture to evaporate and the molecules to break down? Chances are some *roving bovine* will come along and eat it! Particularly good— in fact great—are those disposable plates made of dried leaves. The cows love 'em. Untreated paper—without wax—takes several weeks, sometimes months depending on the quality and weather conditions. Treated paper takes years because the chemicals or wax create a barrier preventing moisture to wick into the cellulose. Did you know that plastic food containers take decades to biodegrade? Plastic is the worst trash, and as modern manufacturing speeds along it has become the preferred package.

We are fanatical about keeping California *squeaky clean*—for several reasons. First the law is so severe—if you get caught throwing trash on the ground in my State you are going to pay a Rs. 42,000 fine for your first offense. The second time you're going to jail *plus* having to pay through the nose. *Ouch!* My small community has a public safety officer, whose job is to ride around the neighborhoods and give citations for *visual blight*— the politically correct way of saying 'you have a lot of crap in your yard – clean it up'. We get a lot of tourist and don't want them to think we live like slobs. Plus—you think the land value is high here—you ought to get a load of the prices on the West Coast. They're astronomical. Ask me—I'm a *grihastra* and you can bet your sweet petunias we want to maintain the highest property value. The houses and yards are immaculate. An Indian friend once said: *It's too perfect.* Wrong. It's not about perfection—it's about *land value*. It's is not only California that polices its trash—all the states do. And, if you think America is clean, Singapore is *double squeaky clean*.

I remember when the federal government launched a national campaign to clean up America. There were many catchy expressions. *Don't Be A Litterbug* was one of the strongest. I always thought *Keep America Clean – Pitch In* was cute. Next to the word *Pitch In* was a trash basket. Of course, government provides abundant opportunities for disposing of trash. Receptacles are everywhere, conveniently placed wherever humans congregate; at bus stations, train stations, public parks and recreation areas. And, you'll find no shortage of well paid workers employed specifically to monitor these areas. Large street cleaning machines roll through the neighborhoods on a scheduled basis, vacuuming and wet sweeping. Why, we've even got dispensers filled with high tech double-lined bags so you can pick up your dog's poop! Bangalore City Planners would do well to take note, and put something similar along the favorite pissing spots for men on their way to work.

A great success was the California Department of Transportation's brainstorm called *Adopt A Highway.* Whoever dreamed up this great idea deserves a bear hug from Arnold Schartzneggar, our *governator.* Any citizen can acquire a stretch of road to keep clean, pay a one time processing fee to the State which in turn has a placard with your name or business (you can include a logo) posted on the roadside. It's a great way to get a lot of advertising, plus the State benefits by having a huge workforce cleaning the roads.

Another cleaver scheme that has been in effect for over 25 years is *court ordered public service.* It used to be only on a volunteer basis but the State wised up. If you have been in trouble—my middle name—the judge may give you an option or order you to work so many hours of community service. Generally, this entails cleaning roadsides that have not been 'adopted' and other public lands. Once, in my wild days, I had a run in with the law—nothing serious—just a little high-speed gun battle. Just kidding, folks!—it was a traffic violation. And, I was ordered to report to work on government land in a remote area. As it turned out there were several badly neglected buildings. When I told them I was a builder and would do their repairs they reduced the number of days in half. In this way I paid my debt to society and they reaped the benefits of my expertise.

Every year a small group of friends organize our own beach clean up. We meet on Sunday morning and after coffee walk a mile or two along the coast—cleaning as we go. If you ever come to California you must visit Monterey—and see how clean I keep the beach. Okay, so I'm not alone. Many other religious groups, schools, and civic organizations do similarly. The whole community is involved in keeping their part of the planet pristine. Unfortunately, not all our neighbors from south of the border have the same high standard of appreciation—or, perhaps Mexico doesn't strictly enforce litter laws so you may find lower income neighborhoods not as nicely maintained. I go as far as to keep a *mechanical grabber*—a handy gadget that eliminates having to stoop over—in the back of my Jeep and will in a heart beat pick up trash. And, not only in my own yard.

I remember our first visit to a medium size town a few hours drive from Bangalore. Debris was stren everywhere. My wife and I went to two different shops—one to get latex gloves, the other for large plastic bags. Then we started at one end of town and worked our way to the other. When we were done we had collect about 6 sacks of trash and had the pleasure of seeing the main street of that picturesque town clean for about 15 minutes. That was how long it took before the shopkeepers and pedestrians started throwing their garbage anywhere and everywhere.

Ask any psychologist about the impact of environment. It is essential. Our surroundings both condition and reflect our mind and mood. When you are in a clean esthetic place your mind automatically gravitates towards *shanti*. Medical healers have become aware of this fact and you will find the new breed of hospitals architecturally esthetic, more like 5-star hotels. What do you suppose the expression *Godliness is cleanliness* means? Why is it when we are clean we're closer to God? I took home something very important from India during one of my earlier visits. From the Hindus. One of the three manifestations of God aspected in the feminine form is called *Lakshmi*—goddess of wealth & prosperity. A wife is called *grihalakshmi* – the goddess of the home. If you want to attract *Lakshmi* it is imperative to keep your house in order. I used to not think twice if crumbs fell on the floor or the bed didn't get made. But, I want Lakshmi to be near and dear, so I make an extra effort to observe the rule of cleanliness. In return, Lakshmi gives me her blessings. Don't take my word for it—try and see for yourself. If you're a City Planner and want to attract crores of foreign investment dollars… Well, just think about it. Do you judge the residents of an estate by the condition of the property? What is reflected outside evidences the condition of the people inside.

The Vedas come from this land called *Matabhuumi*. Let's try harder not to throw trash in Mother's face. I want to hear you say: *Keep Bharat sundar hai.*

෨৵ৎ

When Mr. Butts Make an Ass of You

The American Tobacco Industry

The worst kind of smoker is a reformed one, so they say. And, oh, how I loved to light up. After 30 years of a'huffin''n a'puffin' I started to develop a little cough—even though I didn't have a cold. And, although I never thought of myself as 'athletic' unless you consider table tennis a sport—I did think of myself as physical—somewhere between a workhorse and a pack mule! In those days I was doing a lot of construction, and for any of you who have tried your hand at it you know it's a good workout. Friends used to say, "Why don't we go to the gym," and I'd reply backhanding a bead of sweat away, "Why don't we go to the bar instead and have a couple of cold beers!" *Economy of movement*. The bar room would inevitably be a filled with smokers, each belching out a cloud of smoke like a rickety old bus in Bangalore. Everybody smoked.

Smoking was cool. Society went bonkers over cigarettes. Check out black 'n white Hollywood flicks from the '1930-1950's. They are smoking their heads off. It was glamorous—the beautiful woman in a shimmering gown—split up the side—slipping out of the backseat of a long limousine, one white gloved hand limply extended with a smoldering cigarette in a Mother of Pearl holder. An internationally recognized American icon is the Marlborough Man, a stalwart cowboy, with broad brim Stetson hat, neckerchief, chaps and leather gauntlets, leading a chestnut Morgan Quarter-horse by the reins in one hand, a coiled lariat rope slung over the opposite shoulder, with a cigarette dangling from the corner of his mouth under an endless sky on the lone prairie. The image is a marketer's dream symbolizing the independent macho man. Tobacco companies went so far as to target children conditioning them to want to smoke when they became of age. For me that age was eleven!

Nobody actually likes the taste of cigarettes, even though the smell is very aromatic. A person doesn't just one day wake up, yawn, stretch their arms and say, *What a great day to start smoking. I think I'll light up.* For those who have tried it all will agree that the first puffs cause a great physical reaction—violent coughing is followed by a feeling of dizziness, almost a drunkenness; you start salivating and may feel like vomiting. Let me share a little secret with you. The body is a perfect system but it depends on the mind to take it around and make it do things—like the oxen and driver. When it reacts violently to what it is being given—that's a pretty good sign that whatever it is isn't good for your body. And—pay attention here—what isn't good for your body isn't good for you. *Capish?*

There are two aspects in the pathology of a smoker, habit and addiction. In part, smoking is a *learned behavior* acquired by the mind. Researchers have even trained laboratory rats to smoke and drink whiskey—I understand they're excellent poker players too! What they don't tell you in the study is that the rats are given food as rewards for learning these behaviors. *The things they waste taxpayer's money on!* Another word for a learned behavior is...? You've got it—*habit.* But is smoking only a habit? Now, I hope you're sitting down because what I'm about to tell you may come as a shock too overpowering for your brain circuits. And, I don't want to loose a reader. R.J. Reynolds and Phillip Morris—the two largest producers of cigarettes in the world—conducted clandestine experiments on humans during the later half of the 1930's. They were interested in studying the effects of tobacco on the human system and tried things like *spiking* where as much as four times the amount of nicotine was added to the cigarette. What they discovered in the study is that the nicotine is a highly addictive substance and that the subjects in the experiment experienced the same sort of withdrawal symptoms of heroine addicts! Since the 1930's the tobacco industry knew that cigarettes are not only habit forming—*they're addictive*! If tobacco was just now being introduced to society, the US Food & Drug Administration would prohibit its sale without a medical doctor's written prescription. If you smoke or know someone who does—never refer to smoking as a *habit*—it's an *addiction*. If this isn't bad enough—hang on—it gets worse. The addiction is only half the problem. You don't die from nicotine addiction. What you die from is the tar, a sticky black alkaloid that coats the tiny delicate follicles in the lungs that allow the body to oxygenate with every breath you take. Tar is the killer. For me this knowledge was transformative and I immediately threw the *coffin sticks* out the window. That was fourteen years ago.

You might feel the same sense of outrage and, like me, want to hurt someone! You may ask, "How can anyone knowingly mislead and jeopardize the lives of innocent people?" This is a good question, and you are such a peaceful loving people, *Bharat*, I know it must be hard for you. But the facts are pure and simple, and can be summed up in one word: *Greed*. Do you have any idea of how much profit there is in the sale of one package of cigarettes? Mr. Reynolds and Mr. Morris and the heirs to their imperial fortunes saw a bonanza to be made. They started in America then blew smoke throughout the world. Mr. Butts and his family made an ass out of millions of us. And, when you are as rich as the tobacco families who formed a monopolized corporate cartel—with high paid pit-bull attorneys and alligator lobbyist—there is no way to beat them. They win every time. Almost. Recently, the courts have awarded some damages to longtime smokers. A lot of good a fist full of dollars does when you're knocking at Death's door.

If you are not aware of the dangers of smoking—and by the looks of things most Indians are not—let me dial it in for you, *mera dost.* Cigarette smoking is the forth leading killer in the West causing heart disease, lung cancer, and the disease that starts out as a little cough then ends with oxygen tubes shoved in your nostrils to keep you going—even though you won't be going too far in your wheelchair when you have emphysema. Hello! Are you still there? So insidious are the effects of prolonged tobacco use the Surgeon General, appointed by the President, perceived the consequences and made Congress pass a labeling law that clearly states the hazards and risks.

Now, *Bharat*, you're actually the best—*Numero Uno*—in the world when it comes to teaching others the philosophy of non-violence. *Ahimsa.* Let me ask you this: Can you actually think of doing something more violent to your own body than to purposefully give it a disease that will slowly and painfully end your life? And think of how painful it is for your family to watch you suffer. I want to share something personal with you. A few months ago my dear stepmother had to have her breast removed—a *radical mastectomy.* We had hoped that this would be enough payment for her years of smoking. But, it isn't. They've found more cancer.

Nature has created some awesome wonders in the plant kingdom. Tobacco is one of them. Last year, I drove through Tennessee on my way to Nashville to play a little guitar. Tobacco plants have great beauty; tall majestic stalks with wide golden leaves. And the smell— it's up there with roasted coffee beans or vanilla. I'm sure there must be some grand use for such a wonderful creation—but inhaling the smoldering fumes certainly isn't it! If you really truly feel the urge to smoke—do what I do—light a fragrant stick of incense. Don't let Mr. Butts make an ass out of you.

৵৶

Off The Deep End
Pistol Packing Americans

Have you ever stopped and wondered what mentally triggers a human being, who by all appearances is normal, to suddenly go off the deep end? The West is full of characters in literature and living who have this ballistic Dr. Jeckel & Mr. Hyde personality, toggling between the duality of being cruel and being kind. Of the developed nations America leaves the competition far behind. Have you seen Michael Moore's *Bowling For Columbine*? When Dirty Harry is pointing a high caliber pistol point blank at a man's head, dares him to make the slightest move, threatening: *"Go ahead and make my day"*—he isn't kidding! What kind of sick perverted pleasure can a person find in killing another human being? Ask Jeffry Dalmer.

For those of you who are not familiar with the Northwest's baby-face serial killer, Jeffry was a very bad boy with a perchance for cannibalism. He would entice his young homosexual lovers home—I'm sure it wasn't for cookies and tea—then chemically incapacitate, kill and eat them. Don't ask me how! Probably barbecued or with a curry sauce! Anyway, it sure added a twist to the expression *"having a friend for dinner"*—and of course—a very strong argument for vegetarianism!

You can total the deaths by guns from all the rest of the developed nations and America exceeds that by five times. There were over 7,000 people shot last year. If you stop and consider there are over 30,000,000 privately owned guns in the country it's a relatively low statistic. Neighboring Canada is a large gun owning population but has very few gun-related deaths—54 last year. How do people become so violent? Is it inherent in human personality or is it a learned social behavior?

All mammals have emotions; humans are no different in that respect. We laugh if we see our supervisor getting his butt chewed out by the boss, cry when the finance company repossess our new car for failure to pay the loan, and become furious when our wife charges a staggering debt for clothing at the department store. Is it not so? But, do we want to kill her? (Hey—be sure my wife doesn't read this—but when she bought a piano for Rs 4 lakhs without consulting me, I came close!) And, although our emotions play a key role they are not the main reason people blow their cool. Social conditioning is. How a person reacts to a given situation is largely conditioned by culture. A *conditioned response* is nothing more than a *learned behavior*—a habit. We have the power to discriminate between good habits and bad. However, when your entire society behaves the same way, very few are developed enough to break the mould.

In India while boys are learning to swim, play Tag, and roll tires with sticks boys in America are learning to kill and destroy things. They also learn swimming—usually at home in their own pools—*like I did*—and roll tires with car keys. Now, I'll never forget how happy I was when Santa Claus brought me a *Fanner 50* for my sixth birthday—a beautiful silver revolver with a bone handle grip that fired real plastic bullets. For my ninth birthday I was given a Daisy air gun that shot small copper balls, which were great for killing small creatures—birds and that sort of thing. Then came the Big Day—my first real gun—a Ted Williams. 22 caliber semiautomatic. I couldn't imagine a better gift for an eleven-year-old boy! Regretfully, Mom wouldn't let me play with it in the house, afraid I might accidentally shoot Dad in the head—or even more vital parts. By the time I graduated from high school there weren't too many living things left in the neighborhood—of course, all the other kids had guns too. My girl cousin Maggie thought it was funny letting me shoot her 12-gauge shotgun. She didn't tell me the trick about holding the stock hard against the shoulder and leaning far forward before pulling the trigger. The recoil knocked the daylights out of me! Great fun! The fact is that children in my country witness over 17,000 deaths and acts of violence before the age of five! As the seed so the tree.

I can't begin to tell you what a relief it is to be here, *Bharat*. I am more afraid of being snake bitten or struck by lightening than of being a victim of violent crime. Although you've had your fair share of struggle to "throw off the bit of tyranny", to quote your revolutionary hero, young Aurobindo, and there is still much political tension with Pakistan, the unresolved situation in Kashmir and conflicts with Naxal communists, you are blessed at not having had such a maniacal affair with guns. You set a great example to the rest of the world with your diplomacy and forbearance; yet at a moment's notice the *Nag* and *Trisula* are at your beck and call. I am never fooled by your gentleness, mistaking it for naivete. By example you teach the rest of the world the principles of non-violence. But, let no one interpret your philosophy as a sign of weakness. That would be fatal—because you also teach us *dharma* and I have seen your *Arjunas* and *Arjunis* ready to demonstrate the warrior's oath. When you visit America—please do—don't forget to bring your bulletproof vest. But, if in the haste of packing you do forget—that's okay—I'll lend you one of ours. You'll find a small gun in one of the pockets—I know how difficult it is to carry them on airplanes these days. In America, you never know when you'll need one.

৵৶

How to Eat a Cow
The Biochemistry Of Vegetarianism

Before we begin I feel it only fair to warn you—some of what I'm about to say may make you sick to your stomach, but, probably not any more than some of the programs they show on TV! I grew up in a carnivorous country—carnivorous in more ways than one. Meat was actually, and still is, considered an essential food group (EFG) which means that if you don't eat a scientifically calculated amount of it you will not enjoy good health. Believing this, educators and parents are taught that to be good parents we need to feed our babies meat, and so the tiny tykes are weaned off mother's milk and given cow milk—and of course, pureed pigs, chickens, and by far the most abundant, beef. *Beef in a blender.* I see a new flavor coming for a *lassie!* Americans eat 240 lbs. of beef, 82 lbs. of chicken, and 68 lbs. of pork per year per person. They also eat a lot of sea food and fish even though the Japanese are still the Top Dogs when it comes to sea-kill. When the rest of the world had placed a ban on whaling the Japanese were still slipping a few whales in their hip pocket in the name of 'science'. After killing and weighing the whales and taking minute tissue samples for lab cultures, checking for mercury, the rest of the highly intelligent endangered mammals were slabbed into steaks and sold at phenomenal prices on the open market.

The developed nations have a strong tooth-hold on this notion of animal protein being an EFG even when the fact is there is no scientific evidence supporting the claim. No controlled experiments were ever conducted of raising one group of children on non-meat cuisine and the another as omnivores. I mean—what conscientious parent would actually expose their children to danger? What if the scientists were right! We had a horrible image of a poor little undernourished anemic child, a bag of skin 'n bones, suffering because her parents didn't feed her hamburgers! Instead of looking at nations whose diets consisted mostly of foods other than dead animals we were fed this rasher of lies. I have traveled India stem to stern and found in every corner humans radiating good health, sound mind and exemplary character—okay, there was that one incident with the auto rickshaw driver I'd prefer not to mention, but...! Why do you suppose a government would lie to its own citizens?

Currently the cost of one pound—a little under a half kilo—of ground sirloin costs about $3.25. At a slaughter weight of 800 lbs. a butchered steer—the breed most commonly raised—is worth $2,600 per animal. The Mac Donald corporation boosts that it has served over 18 billion ¼ lb. hamburgers. Anybody got a calculator?!? The bottom line is that beef is big business. A nighttime satellite fly over Central and South America shows the glowing lights from small fires of poor *slash and burn* farmers eking out a hand-to-mouth living, deforesting the rain forest to allow green pasture to grow in order to raise beef for their ravenous northern neighbor—the United States. It is a bankrupt farming practice that destroys habitat, endangering both flora and fauna. The land also erodes in one or two seasons and the rivers are choked with the red soil.

In developing nations when a family's income increases what is the first thing that changes in their lifestyle? Their diet. And, what is the first dietary thing that increases? The consumption of meat. With more than ten years of NAFTA we have seen the new Chinese middleclass changing their eating habits, which evermore resembles the West. Chinese favorite meat is pork. It takes 900 lbs. of grain to raise a pig to a slaughter weight of 240 lbs.—enough protein for 45 days. Whereas the 900 lbs. of grain would last for 13 months!

Have you ever asked yourself "Why did the high priests want to kill Lord Jesus?" If you're a Christian you may vehemently disagree with me, but one school of thought asserts there were multiple issues but most certainly a major issue would have been because he publicly denounced the sacrificial slaughter of animals to God for religious holidays. Guess who had the exclusive right to selling sacred animals? The priests. And, guess what was one of their greatest sources of revenue?

With 700 million, India has the largest vegetarian population in the world. It is imperative that the rest of the world learns this philosophy of vegetarianism. If for no other reason than to protect the planet from the growing number of carnivores. Already the 15% who live in the developed nation who can afford meat, have depleted huge numbers of the ocean's game fish; creatures like crabs, lobsters, prawns and shrimp are becoming scarcer as trawling ships rake metal catch-screens across the ocean floors destroying the environment with impunity. The other 85% of the planet's economically developing population will be following China's example unless taught otherwise.

For thousands of years India has had knowledge of the biochemistry of food. During the times of Lord Krishna the *gunas* were defined and the different energetic qualities of food spelled out. We can see the effectiveness of this cause and effect chemistry. Works like *Holy Science* by Sri Yukateswar make powerful arguments in favor of non-meat alternatives. Vegetarianism makes you a gentle, less aggressive people. The agitated Western diet breeds more disease in both senses of the word. I see it.

And talk about delicious! *Bharat*—you have evolved your own distinctive cuisine known throughout the world. I have eaten *chapati* in London, and have favorite Indian restaurants in San Francisco and Monterey. I can buy *Tandoori nan* at any large grocery store. You do things with vegetables that most of us have never imagined; *samosa* and *kofta*, puffs and *pakoras*, curries and *masalas*. Your *rasam* is awesome! Recently, I was talking with a dietary specialist about India's culinary mastery. Take rice for example. In the States we only know how to boil it. Some chefs have learned from the Italians how to make pilaf, a seasoned rice cooked in a pan with vegetables. The Chinese are more versatile but still limited. My nutritionist prepared rice with cumin, lemon rice, *pilau*, *briannyi*, curd rice, sweet rice, ghee rice, *appam*—each day she had a different dish. There are many rice cultures in the world but remember—your culture is the oldest. Some of these recipes go back to the dawn of civilization. You're still cooking with the same fire. We can market you as the Guru Of Grub in a culinary epic titled the *Maha-paratha*!

Now—I did promise to tell you how to eat a cow. Every good carnivore knows the answer to that question—one hamburger at a time! And, if you see any Texans walking around licking their chops—perhaps they're probably feasting their eyes on some of those prime heifers I've seen roaming the city streets as if nobody owned them.

�❧�

A Cup of Tea
India's Gift to Civilization

Bharat, you have mastered many arts—the art of classical music, drama and dance in a system uniquely your own; timeless philosophy, Tamil poetry, and fine cuisine, again quite distinctive. Undeniably, many are your cultural gifts. But, perhaps the greatest and most humble of these cultural gifts, and one most of you take it for granted, is that elixir of the Gods—black milk tea or—*chai*.

It strikes me as rather curious that India doesn't make a big deal out of drinking tea—perhaps you're missing a *scoring opportunity*. Why not? England, who stole—excuse me—misappropriated and monopolized your delicious gift to the world, also made *high tea* a ritual culturally synonymous with snobbish dignity. So complete was the assimilation of tea as a symbol of The Empire that most people in the world still think of England as the birthplace of black tea. My own countrymen sent them packing in 1774 when the Brits tried taxing the American colonist who revolted by boarding their ship in the night and dumping the cargo of tea into the Boston harbor. After 200 years the bay still looks like a giant bowl of tea!

The Japanese also elevate tea to a sacred role and, along with rice, is associated with their most 'sanc-*tea*-monious' rituals. No wedding or prayer would be complete without sipping a bit. Same with the Chinese. In restaurants you do not order tea—the waiter brings a pot automatically when coming to your table with menus. And—have you ever tasted their tea? That thin green watery brew called *oolong?* Hey—what can I say?!? Waiter—make mine a *chai, kripaya.*

For those with creative myopia I'll share a vision. When it comes to ritual, *Bharat,* you are at least two laps ahead of the nearest competitor. Have you ever seen a *puja* or *homa* or how they celebrate *Deepavali?* Talk about ritual. And if that doesn't get your propeller spinning—how about some of your national observances—like *Ganesh Chaturthi*—a four day long ritual. Not, satisfied? Try *Navaratri.* I see India adding a tea ritual to the current itinerary. It's doable. A man and woman, perhaps invited guests, put on traditional Indian clothing, *saris, jubbahs, kurtas, longhis, punjabis*—you must have seen these. Try wearing them. Then *agrabati* is lit and placed in a nice holder. A recording of classical flute or raga augments the ambiance. The tea is brewed patiently, giving the man and woman time to catch up on the days events. Then it is served in special cups—not these stainless steel tumblers that look like they came from a hospital and blister your fingers and lips! You've got fabulous potters here. Use them. After giving thanks for the earth's abundance the couple relaxes, each appreciating the other's company while enjoying the fruit of your own nation. *I'm fishing for an invitation.*

To learn to brew a perfect cup of *chai* required a trip to Ooty. However, I don't recommend that you go there—the fresh air might damage your lungs. The beauty might hurt your eyes. As the vehicle ascended higher the air chilled and the moisture increased. Far below lay little hamlets and villages dotting the quilted farmland. Bands of rhesus monkeys watched with curiosity as the car passed. Then the forested canopy opened and tea terraces mushroomed. Small family plots quickly graduated into large commercial plantations. Arriving at my destination, I was greeted by M.K. Venkateswar who escorted me down a meandering pathway to a modest adobe house with a palm thatched roof not visible from the road. I joined Venkateswar sitting on the floor in *padmasana* while he made *chai* from a patented family recipe *bahut purana hai.*

Brewing a perfect cup of tea. Of course the tea we love slurping the most is *Chaykada*—black tea from Kerala. And, it comes in two popular beverages – *masala (spiced) chai* or *dudhwala chai* – milk tea. Leaves picked at one or six months determine the quality and price. You also have a couple of other varieties—the long leaf Darjeeling from the North which is delicate and floral, and the *Sulaimani* whose acquaintance I have not made but understand is quite nice—black and lemony. Milk tea is pretty straightforward. Bring a cup of milk to a boil, being careful not to let it boil over, add a teaspoon of tea, steep 5-6 minutes, sweeten to taste. To make *masala chai* I use a liquid base of 60% water 40% whole milk. Into the boiling water I add 2-4 slices of ginger, depending on my mood, 2 pods of cardamom cracked open, 2-3 cloves, a piece of cinnamon, a pinch of *saunf* or anise seed per person; sometimes I add a few black pepper corns. (You'll find the combination of pepper and ginger is a great homeopathic remedy for alleviating a sore throat.) At home I have a stone mortar & pestle and love "bruising the spices" to release their aromatic essence. Simmer 15 minutes. Add 1 ¼-1 ½ teaspoons of black *chaykada*—make sure it's a *tea-spoon*. Let steep 6 minutes. Add the milk and carefully bring the brew to a boil. Strain and serve hot.

I will let you in on a little secret most folks overlook—*teacher* is a compounded word, not unlike Sanskrit words that often convey deeper meanings – such as, *bhajan* which most people think of as an India spiritual song, but actually means *bha = god + jnana = to know.* I'm a singer, not a semanticist. Still, you don't have to be a rocket scientist to figure it out! Obviously, the word *teacher* means *tea,* the very subject we're talking about + *cher* from *cherish.* A *teacher* is someone who *cherishes tea.* (And, you wonder why they call me *Kipacharya?!*)

This country has many great things to teach the rest of the world. Stop importing the tawdry tinsel and trash from Western nations and export your own brand of 'civilization'. *Bharat,* own up to who you are. Tea isn't British—it's Indian. You will be pleased to know, you can go to any coffee or tea shop in the West and find *chai* in many variations on the menu. Toast this idea and say, *"I'll drink to that."*

Undressing a Nation
Timeless Indian Fashions

I liked it the first time I saw it—but didn't know what to call it—a loose fitting sheet wrapped around a man in such a way to make billowy pant legs, and pleated in front in such a way to create a majestic cascade of cotton. Then he whipped his oxen's haunches and moved on down the dusty village avenue. I had just had my first introduction to a timeless Indian fashion—the *dhoti*.

The oldest portrayals of the Krishna avatar, circa 3,500 BC, show him wearing a *dhoti* or perhaps a *lungi,* a slightly shorter garment. The technical differences between them is about two meters, the *dhoti* being four meters—and fabric color; the *dhoti* is generally a solid color with a decorative border, while the *lungi* comes in more patterns than you can shake a stick at. A third garment, the two meter knee length *suti,* is a household garment amongst the majority of the rural population. Egyptian hieroglyphs show men wearing wrap-arounds. Rama is much older and often depicted with both an elaborate *dhoti* and cummerbund tied around the waist. When a modern person wears either garment a direct connection is established with India's cultural heritage—which many of us know, is the common heritage of humans on the planet.

Thousands of travelers pulsate through Bangalore Railway Station daily in their own worlds and orbits. So, I was a bit taken back when one trip to Chennai, still Madras at that time, I was accosted by several men, who broke the boundary of personal concern to come over and chat with me. Each remarked on how nice the traditional clothing of their countrymen looked—even on a *gori videsh.* I noticed all of them were wearing Western garb in spite of the fact the thermometer was shooting off the scale! What is this fascination with other people's gardens when your own is laden with fruit? *Bharat*, you need not feel shame or think traditional Eastern clothing is a sign of provincialism or that it casts dispersions on your evolutionary level. The fact is you live in an equatorial zone. The relaxed loose fitting garments allow the air to circulate and keeps the skin cooler, and for men, according to a theory of my college psychology professor—it helps maintains our reproductive organs at a consistent temperature. Okay! So the guy was a little weird! When you reject your cultural heritage not only does it severe the tie with the past, you maybe shooting yourself in the foot by overlooking an important *economic scoring opportunity.*

Whether you know it or not at present there is a fashion craze among Western teenage girls. They are wearing *cholis* which they call *halters*, perhaps not realizing the design comes from classical Indian fashion. I hope you're sitting down—it's just the *choli* without the *chuni!* The *hot look* is a pair of pants so tight they look painted on and a skin tight *choli*—that's it. Regretfully, the *hot look* is why American teenage girls lead the developed nations in teen pregnancy! One of you young marketing Turks could make a killing if you crack the designer label nut—and market *cholis* in traditional design patterns. Americans love stuff from India—plus appreciate the lower retail prices.

Of course, for those of you who are unaware, the *sari* is a national icon synonymous with India. Anywhere you travel in the world when you see a *sari* the person wearing it can only be from one place. If you're ever in the Bangalore and want to score some points with your sweetie, you will find the very classy *chudidar*, a pegged pajama pant with a knee length *kurta* blouse coming in a myriad of colors and patterns. Worn with a coordinated *chuni* or *dupatta* covering the bosom, they start in the hundreds and run into thousands of rupees.

59

And, while we're on the subject let's not overlook the *Punjabi*— a baggy pajama pant with a long *kurta* shirt for men. When worn with *chappels*, open toed sandals, these loose fitting fashions are extremely comfortable. I own several *Punjabis* and when I wear them in the West—heads turn. True story: I was traveling in a *Punjabi* leaving India flying to visit my wife's family in the Mediterranean. We landed in Budapest, Hungary only to discover our luggage had gone on to Paris, France. The airline promised to do everything possible to recover our bags. Meanwhile stuck in Budapest, we made arrangements to rent a room in a flat. "*Are you shooting a movie?*" the landlady asked, eyeing me up and down as I eased out of the taxi. "*I'm certain I've seen you on television before in that same outfit.*" I assured her I wasn't a big shot and lied a little, "*Many men dress like this in India.*" But, there was no convincing her. So I just gave her an autograph and let it go at that!

If you've been imprisoned in Western clothes all your life—buy some Eastern threads and get out of jail! In the Global Village you're allowed to wear a *lungi, thobe,* or *Levi's 501's*. Haven't you heard, *Bharat?*— "It's all good". But when you habitually copy and paste fashions and styles that are not your own, overlooking the potential wealth in your own cotton fields you're missing a *scoring opportunity*. So let's get cracking—crack out the sketchbooks, crack out the E-Bay websites—crack me out a *cocojal* while you're at it. And, should any of you designers have some samples—I know one dude who loves your duds!

❧

Abraham Lincoln of India
Measuring by a Different Yardstick

A few years back, I was traveling with my wife in the European country, Montenegro, which is in the throes of a national reformation since the breakup of former Yugoslavia and the expulsion of Slobodan Milosovic. A disc jockey from one of the local radio stations invited me to talk on her show. The topic was my impressions of her country. In the ensuing time, as I was scoring more kilometers on my Around The World membership card, I had many opportunities to talk to Montenegrin citizens. Besides the economy, which is shot to hell – I've got a bank note worth 500,000,000,000 dinars which could buy about a half dozen eggs! – the biggest complaint was trust in the leadership. After a guy like Milosovic, who was stealing money from the treasury by the truckload, who can blame them. I asked many people if they thought there were any countrymen the caliber of Abraham Lincoln. None believed there was a single soul among them with the integrity and leadership dynamic of 'Honest Abe'. I even talked to parents with a gifted son working on a Ph.D. in political science; he wasn't interest in the job!

When I asked the same question in India—many people said, "Certainly. There are many. And, why use Lincoln as a yardstick?" *Don't you just hate it when they get uppity with you!* So, I set out on my own quest to see what I could find out. And, they were right. Great leaders have been here and are here now.

Packing a bag, I hopped a train bound for Pondicherry, Tamil Nadu to investigate the claim a giant had left footprints on the golden pages of history. I left that place satisfied with my finding. Before his spiritual awakening Aurobindo Gosh (1872-1950) was a firebrand. Sent abroad by his father, a medical doctor, Aurobindo and two older brothers studied in England. The lad proved his superior intellect, scoring exceptionally well at Ivy League institutions in Cambridge. Upon completing his formal education, Gosh was for all intents and purposes an Englishman. He didn't speak a lick of Hindi nor any of India's 25 other major languages. Returning to Bengal at the turn of the Twentieth Century, Aurobindo quickly became immersed in the nationalistic revolutionary tide drenching the nation. After 300 years of British imperialism India was finally fed up. Tension mounted everywhere. As he discovered his cultural heritage and true identity Aurobindo's resentment toward British colonialist, gori videshis, exploiting his countrymen for centuries grew. That great intellect began charting a course leading to a distant goal of national independence. In a few short years after arriving in a country – a homeland – he had never known Aurobindo rose to prominence as a revolutionary mastermind and mouthpiece, articulating anarchistic messages through various publications, advocating active and passive resistance. The latter concept Mohandas Gandhi would evolve to perfection. Considered a public enemy, the British Raj looked for any excuse to arrest the rebel rouser and finally nailed him on trumped up charges of sabotage. The trouble maker landed in solitary confinement. Conspiring against the British government constituted treason punishable by death. Gosh faced a serious court battle in which the prosecution resorted to low blows and underhanded tactics. Just when all seemed lost, the brilliant efforts of his defense attorney overturned the trial and won Gosh's freedom. But, his troubles weren't over. Two more assassination attempts by the British failed. Eventually, the calling of a spiritual life weaned him away from politics and Aurobindo Gosh went on to becoming one of the most recognized evolutionary philosophers of modern times. Classes devoted exclusively to his major writings are taught at universities throughout the world. When I see young people everywhere venerating iconic Che Guevara, the martyred revolutionary pre-med student from Argentina, I can't help to think they are truly missing one of the greats – young Aurobindo Gosh. At his residence in Pondicherry I saw his shadow impetuously pacing in the upstairs study and thought long and hard about his commitment, conviction and contribution.

Heading further south, with a few asides at Chitambaram and Madurai, I was soon stepping down from the train in Rameshawaram. After visiting the temple and being consecrated with 22 *tirthams* an auto took me to a small beach south of Dhanushkodi. Following a swim in the warm crystal blue ocean, which impressed the local fisherman (give a guy a break—what do you think coastal Californians do all day long?!), we returned to town. The driver mentioned that President Abdul Kalam was from this place and his family home was on the way. So, we stopped at the House of Kalam where I met the President's affable older brother, who still resides there. But, it wasn't until I read *Wings Of Fire,* Kalam's biography, that I actually appreciated the caliber of this man's character. I am not a scientist so I cannot speak to his technical accomplishments. But I am passionate about life and recognize and respect those among us who stand on the shoulders of giants in order to catch a glimpse of the future. Mr. Kalam saw India's future and refused to allow anything to prevent its unfoldment. From a young age Kalam made tremendous personal commitments and sacrifices, giving up *grihastra* family and householder life. He married *Bharat.* He believed his countrymen could raise to any challenge in science. He refused to kowtow to the superpowers wanting to monopolize technology. He forged ahead where others flaked out. He licked his wounds when the talons of failure threaten the dream of putting India in outer space. He encountered defeat with renewed optimism. He taught the astute observer that tenacity is the key to success. And, when the highest laurels a grateful nation can bestow upon one of its own were presented, he accepted the praise with humility always reverent to the motivating Spirit.

I asked if there were any Abraham Lincolns in India and was told "Abdul Kalam is one." And, when I went to see with my own eyes—you were right—we make a big mistake by using Western heroes as a yardstick. They are dwarfed by some of the giant personalities here on your own native soil. *Bharat*, quit running after your neighbors. I've been saying allong, we all want what you have and come great distances at considerable expense to get just a little taste of it. You are a unique nation. Be proud of your accomplishments but don't linger long. A glorious future is hanging on the horizon. Now is the time for concerted efforts and your best to come forward to the helm. Every ship needs a captain.

One Bad Apple Spoils the Bunch
Corruption in Politics

Everywhere I go in India I keep hearing the same complaint—"Leaders are so corrupt here" or "Judges take bribes" or "Elected officials are stealing public funds". Just the other day, I was told that our domestic worker was paid Rs. 500 for a politician's vote in her village. (Her only regret was that elections weren't held more often—like once a week!) The stories you hear are incredible. And, the fact you hear so many lends credence to the probability that there is some truth to the accusations.

Elected officials, of all a nation's citizens, have the greatest duty—to serve the constituents that put them in office. *Public servants* should be exactly that – servants – and never allowed to serve themselves at the expense of their masters – the public. In a representative government they are the instruments of change and progress. They are lawmakers and should be held accountable for also being law enforcers, always upholding the public trust. They are the ears of the people, listening to the complaints and implementing solutions. They are the eyes of the people seeing what the problems are and working to resolve them. They are the visionaries that carry the society forward so it may enjoy the fruits of its collective efforts. Their qualifications should be good intellect, good management abilities with track records, good communication skills, the knack to resolve conflicts, but above all, the highest caliber of character. One thing that greatly impressed me living in Saudi Arabia, was Arab integrity. They hold family honor as *sacred* and would rather be put to death than to have any stain cast upon their family's name. Once upon a time the

Bharatiya sanskriti, the ancient cultural of *Bharat*, upheld the same noble ideals. (See: Gurudev's Message.)

Why does corruption hurt us? When we pay off judges and representatives of the law we allow the interests of a few to be promoted over the interest of the many. When corruption is allowed to run rampant the society back-slides instead of advancing. Recently, certain public officials in charge of correcting test scores were caught red-handed accepting bribes from students!—which creates a very dangerous precedent, if for no other reason, by promoting the young hoodlums, rewarding their budding corruption with advancement.

When you allow the bacteria of corruption to incubate it becomes a plague that destroys the very foundation of society. You give yourself a black eye and shoot yourself in the foot. Quickly, you earn an international reputation of being crooks. Foreign investors think twice before doing business with you. The citizens of other nations are informed and discouraged from visiting. Like a woman who has lost her virtue, no respectable person would knowingly consort with you. Can India afford a bad reputation at this critical historical juncture?

Billions are funneled into the private coffers of crooks. When President Bush invaded Iraq they found a shipping container with $800 million dollars—stolen by Sadam's son. The Chief of Police of Mexico City, Antonio Juarez, owns several mansions, including a villa with a racetrack, in addition to owning the world's second largest private collection of antique automobiles! *His salary is $60,000 a year!* When you steal money from a rich man—you can empty his wallet—but like a sweetwater well it refills effortlessly. When you steal money from a poor man—not only do you negate years of hard work—you hurt his family too! Can India afford to let its hard earned public funds be pilfered by rodents and crows?

Our friend Cheryl, was dating her boss, Willy Conrad, a high ranking official in the US federal government's Dept. of Immigration, who certified the documentation of people applying for residency—

green cards. I had met him on several social occasions and he struck me as rather *too cool*—pierced ear, dripping with gold, a jet-setter with a Platinum Master Card. I wasn't surprised to read on the front page of the San Francisco Chronicle that the FBI had arrested Willy and where holding him without bail for selling green cards to Chinese immigrants at $10-20,000 a pop. And had been for nine years. *Talk about trouble.* Not only did Willy get a long prison term—ten years—they also cleaned his clock, confiscating all his assets, his bank accounts, his several fine homes, sports cars—oh, yeah—the 65 foot yacht at his Caribbean getaway!

For society to run smoothly the citizens must have an elevated standard of values, such as the Saudis, who would rather die than to have any dispersions cast upon their family honor. People must be encouraged to live morally—or *murali*—as they say up North! And, government must have a system of law enforcement that polices itself. Who guards the guards? Power should never be given without a means to counter balance it. Penalties must be stiff and enforced. No *dakshina.* And if an elected official is found guilty of corruption they must be severely punished—not just slapped on the wrist and set free to continue victimizing people. *Bharat*, you've suffered this indignity long enough. Perhaps you should revive a few archaic punishments from the dusty law books of the past. For minor infractions, the public official—say the Mayor of Bangalore—would be hauled to Ulsoor Park, clamped in a wooden stock and flogged numerous times—ten lashes for goofing off—twenty lashes for not getting key infrastructure projects completed on schedule. Getting caught with your hand in the cookie jar—tax revenue your community has entrusted to your safekeeping—would require you be taken to a hospital where your hand would be surgically removed—just like they still do today in Saudi Arabia. *Stoning* was a great group activity—a little excessive, but very effective and quite an aerobic workout! *Trolling* was mainly used by seafaring captains—dragging you behind a slow moving boat in shark-infested waters. *Drawn & Quartered*—an English favorite, could be called *parceling* in India where the government official's arms and legs are tied to four *Bajajs*— better use *Nandis* for this one—and drive off slowly in different directions. *I'll bet that hurts!* But, it doesn't hurt nearly as much as the pain corrupt government officials cause the public they serve.

≈≈

Root of Evil
Gurudev's Message

Ardha Kumbamela, the largest congregation of people on the planet, attracted an estimated 15 million people this year. Most of them holy men and women and their followers. Disguised as a *kisan* I infiltrated the holy precincts and stayed with my *parivar* from Haridwar, Sri Gurudev Swami Shivananda and the Matri Sadan ashram.

For the years I've known Gurudev I've always been keen on his messages, which are both spiritual and practical. On occasion I have referred to him as General Gurudev because of his adamant stance on irreconcilable issues that compromise the Vedic traditions and laws of society. With 30 years of *tapas* under his belt—or, *dhoti*—he has attained a high level of yoga proficiency and is loved and respected by many people who personally know him. As my Hindi is *bahut buri bate* for some time I had been hoping Gurudev would publish his discourses in English. One day I discovered the Kumbha registration tent doubled as a book store. And, therein to my delight was an English translation of a series of discourses given by Gurudev at a seminar on World Environment Day in Uttarkhand. Right away I saw the work needed the benefit of a native English reader, as the corrections were numerous, and I had an editing assignment!

One of India's greatest challenges is to elevate the leadership and people who are vested with public trust to a mind set where they will follow the tradition of *dharma*, whose roots trace back to Manu. Before sharing the salient points of Gurudev's message I will shock you with a little history of the charismatic *swami* and his dedicated *sannyasis*. Did you know the Ganges River is protected by law?

According to Vedic tradition, bathing in her water is a spiritual baptism. As the Matri Sadan property adjoins the river, and Gurudev performs daily ablutions in the morning and *arati* at sunset—the river is literally a major artery in his life. In Dec. 1999 he filed a formal complaint, noting that a mining company was violating the law, digging up and polluting the river. His formal complaint to local authorities went unheeded. He continued to levy accusations that the mining company, was violating the law, and charged the public officials with performing their duties. Thugs from the company offered the swami money in progressively increasing amounts to withdraw the complaint, but he refused to compromise. One day in January 2000, several policemen showed up at Matri Sadan ashram, forced entry into his house, wearing shoes, rudely interrupted his meditation, and arrested the holy man. Immediately, the Matri Sadan monks started a food fast, which would continue 68 days! A doctor I spoke with and whose house I visited told me that after being in jail for awhile Gurudev became ill. Surreptitiously, hair and fingernail clippings were sent to a French laboratory for independent analysis. The doctor and Matri associates were stunned when the reports came back. Gurudev had extremely high amounts of arsenic in his body— enough to kill the average person! The jailers were poisoning him. The doctor and other close associates were amazed at the saint's yoga power. When New Delhi got wind of the case newspaper articles appeared and upper echelon politicians got into the act. Bye and bye the thing was sorted out. The multimillion-dollar mining operation was ordered to go packing with a boot on the butt in the form of a hefty fine. Furthermore, three top political officials, bribed stooges for the mine, were beheaded from their official duties. Eventually, the river restored itself.

What I learned from studying Gurudev's discourse made perfect sense to me, and hence I am passing it along to you. India is one of the oldest, if not the oldest, developed culture. At a time when Europeans were living in caves, wearing animal skins, and eating grubs and tubers India was making great strides in medicine, civil engineering, mathematics, astronomy, agriculture, art, poetry and governance. Men like Ashok were not merely giants—they were epicenters. What was done thousands of years ago still finds relevance today. Example: please take a paper rupee note – it does not matter if it is a new note with Mahatma Gandhi gracing it or an older one. The lion figures you see on the note is the top of Ashok Pillar and dates back over 2,000 years! I have seen this national treasure at Sarnath and can assure you it is one of the finest carvings in all the world. Now, if you've finished with the rupee note I am taking a collection!

In the days before India was invaded society was well defined by law. Rulers as well as subjects valued their history and tradition. In olden times when a ruler was facing some difficult problem and had to make an important decision but could not clearly see the best solution, rather than take a *weg*—wild educated guess—they summoned their gurus, yogis, astrologers, seers and saints. Schooled in the science of *yoga*—in *kriya* and *raja*—the saints would enter deep meditation and using their yogic power, transcend *maya* and *manas* to arrive at clear solutions. The leaders of India have forgotten mahatmas still exist, preserving the ancient science of religion—yoga. The modern consensus in India is that yoga is superstition—a Harry Potter fantasy. Some of us know better and have seen things *"that made a true believer of me..." Vitamin G.*

Yesteryear people lived regulated lives and followed *dharma*. The average citizen would not think of going against *dharma*; a ruler would rather die a thousand deaths than to break its law. Lord Rama is the classic exemplar for youth of all nations, a perfect person, married at age 16, and suffered and sacrificed until age 30 to keep not a promise he made, rather, a promise his father made! A king's word was law. And a son's duty was to uphold his father's honor, even unto death.

Men have forgotten honor; they have forgotten duty and *Bharatiya sanskriti*; they have forgotten their national identity. Like monkeys pilfering a neglected fruit cart elected officials stuff their pockets from the public coffers, grabbing the hard earned fruits of the people they serve. In the news recently we read India was rated as one of the most corrupt countries in the world. *Bharat,* you have no idea how devastating a blemish that is to your reputation—and how undeserving it is for the majority of the hardworking honest citizens. Reports like this red flag the nation. Like a quarantine, it warns the international business community to keep its distance—keeping at arm's length what is best for your development. Sure people will do business with you—on their terms, not yours. Elected officials and people in leadership positions should be held accountable, fined severely, imprisoned, and in cases of treason, punished according to the law.

On Independence Day, I was traveling by train and discussing politics with students. One bright young lady pointed out that the Constitution of the United States had been amended 28 times in about 225 years whereas the Constitution of India has been changed 94 times in only 58 years. "Why is that?" she asked. Having just finished reading Gurudev's discourse the answer was ready. "Because you've borrowed so much from other cultures and haven't included enough of your own unique identity." Change is a reflection of progress; likewise, tradition is a hallmark of stability. When a thing reaches perfection it stops changing. 500 years of foreign occupation has buried the traditional culture of *Bharat* beneath layers of other people's ideologies. Corruption will stop when India remembers and embraces her heritage and spiritual tradition that puts *dharma* first and individual desires second.

చేం

Race to Zero Point
Alternative Energy Sources

Whether you know it or not there's a world race on. The one who crosses the finish line first will change the balance of power. I had a vision of India winning. As you all know, the world wants energy devices; we want dishwashers (even though my wife still works pretty good!), washing machines, refrigerators with juice and ice dispensers, garbage disposers, microwave ovens, and everything that is remotely remote—if you know what I mean. In my country these things are standard household items. A typical house is wired with 220 volts and 120 amps. It is a fact that Americans consume twice as much energy as their cousins in Europe and one hundred times more than their cousins in India—I know—*been there; done that!*

The things I left at home in California are headed this way right now on a ship called Destiny and will be arriving shortly. India has already started getting ready. Many alternative sources of energy are currently under development. Technologies like biomass degradation are generating electricity in some rural areas. Venkampalli in A.P. is producing 20,000 MV, which serves about 100 households. Of all the byproducts captured by efficient waste management the trophy goes to the Japanese who are experts in converting societal waste into building materials. Although I've never been in a house constructed with these materials I can imagine how they smell!

Let me share something with you. January 2005, I traveled through the central and western states of Mexico and was very impressed with how well Mexicans are capitalizing on one of their greatest natural resources besides the *tortilla*—solar energy. I stayed at hotels and ate at restaurants powered entirely by solar electric.

India currently puts the sun to work—I've seen dear *dhobiwalas* using 'solar dryers'! By far the biggest application to date is the use of solar water heaters. An estimated one million square meters of water is heated nationally. I am currently having a system installed at my place in Whitefield at a cost of Rs.32K. It's a bit pricey and out of reach for the minions. The technology for solar electric cells is another fruit high on the tree. With as many engineers as this country graduates you'd think India could build a better mousetrap. Cheap photo-voltage would help win the race. Maybe a nano or two would give you the oomph.

There's been a lot of huff and puff about harnessing wind. Look before you leap. Don't do what we did in California. Altamonte Pass used to have beautiful rolling hills with milk cows grazing on sweet grass. The milk cows and grass are still there but the whole area is disfigured with ugly metal towers sporting huge airplane propellers. *Visual blithe* is the politically correct term for *ugly*. India currently has a huge wind farm in Tamil Nadu; the entire countryside is sprouting turboprops. Ask yourself—how far did the Dutch ever go with windmills?!?

Nuclear reactors crank out lots of power, and the Tarapur Facility in Maharashtra, the largest in India, generates 540 MWe, and is right up there with any G-8 country. *Applause is in order*. However, there is a dark side to nukes. We've seen what happens when the reactor core melts through its containment. Can the world afford another Chernobyl? And, what to do with the depleted uranium rods that continue to spew deadly radiation for thousands of years?

Inventors are currently playing with new toys. Have you seen Troy Reed's magnetic car? It requires no gas, no oil, no water, no electricity, goes about 60 kph and lasts five years per charge. *How do you like them apples?* Brian DePalma is another maverick who gets his jollies making turbines spin. This great thinker was pooh-poohed by the Establishment for his out-of-the-box ideas. India's own super scientist Mr. Tewari is considered a guru of *over unity physics*. He's another *spin master* and I've seen his little free-energy motor doing its *Tandava*. Hydrogravidics uses relative atmospheric density to turn turbines and there are many home tinkers hoping to be the first to knock on the patent office door with the invention that will change the world. *We're so close.* The real obstacle is not finding mechanical devices but overcoming government policies and corporate wealth that have historically controlled available technology.

When talking about the politics of energy, which I will at greater lengths next time we meet, I always like to cite Nikola Tesla who counted Albert Einstein, Mark Twain, and Max Plank among his friends—Thomas Edison among his enemies. Offer your *pranams* every time you use electricity, thanking Tesla for giving us alternating electric current (the method electricity is delivered worldwide), radio, AC motors, florescent lights, and remote control to name but a few of his prolific inventions. But, when Tesla tried giving the world wireless transmission of electric energy—guess what? The Big Boys who were investing in copper mines said *No way, Bombay!* The invention was suppressed and ultimately forgotten, archived in a cardboard box along with the rest of the inventor's notes in the FBI's basement. Let's have a moment of silence while we contemplate the gravity of what the loss of this single invention meant for the world. Can you imagine cities not spaghettied with power lines and land not devastated by strip-mining? Should technology serve society or should it serve the rich?

Wealth follows politics. We have observed how legislation can be influenced by wealth. When Howard Hughes proposed transatlantic commercial passenger flights for his company American Airlines, a senator with one hand in Juan Trip's hip pocket tried passing a law to secure for Trip's company, Pan American Airlines, the exclusive rights to all international flights. Fortunately, Hughes prevailed.

If the great minds of this country can develop new energy technologies that are *environmentally dharmic* as well as *universally affordable*, and if the government takes a leading role to prevent the monopolization of intellectual property, India will not only win the race but emerge as the newest superpower. *Namaste.*

Building a Better Mousetrap
The Politics of Fossil Fuel

Kogi Indians are little known outside the periphery of their environment in the craggy Andes Mountains of Columbia, South America. Tribal shamans, who believe they are the big brothers and guardians of the planet, are trying to get an important message to us. For the past decade they have observed their *apu*—a sacred mountain, which in their creation myth is the place God first made humans—is sick. The mountain has a fever. Since the beginning of time, according to Kogi, their *apu,* at an elevation of 12,000 kilometers, has been snow-clad. In recent times that white mantle has sweated away. An elder spokesman for the tribe said, "When our scared *apu* is sick the whole world is in great danger."

For the past 35 years scientist have watched and warned while observing a steady rise in the world's temperature. Global warming due to greenhouse gases is no longer a theory but a certifiable fact. Of course, the real danger is not so much the ambient temperature and if we should wear long sleeves or short sleeves, but the ocean's changing thermohaline (TCH)—the salt content in sea water. The saltier the water the cooler it is, the slower the ocean currents—the primary factor for planetary weather. Our oceans are drowning in fresh unsalted water.

I don't want to rock your world but the truth of the matter is that it's too late to undo the cumulative effect of hydro-fluorocarbon pollution. There is no recalling Larsen A and B—two massive chunks of ice the size of Goa that calved off Antarctica last year. For the first time in recorded history ships can sail thorough a northern passage.

A glimpse of the fossil record shows the planet has had a fluctuating temperate past. As recently as 10,000 years ago North America was buried beneath a sheet of ice two kilometers thick at its trailing edge. But, this is the first time in planetary history where human activity has had a direct impact on creating an imbalance. Possibly, what we are witnessing is another ice age in the making.

Now that I've told you the bad news—here's the worst part—human greed is directly to blame. I hope you're sitting down because what I'm about to tell you will floor you. Do you remember Charles Pough? *Of course not!* His great contribution to the world was snuffed out like a stick of incense in a dynamite factory! In 1936 Mr. Pough drove a gas-guzzling 8-cylinder Cadillac from Florida to the US Patent Office, showed the clerks his odometer reading and fuel tags, defiantly put his hands on his hips and said, *How do you like me now?!?* Somewhat confused the clerks did some quick calculations and were astonished to find Pough's carburetor got over 55 miles to the gallon! For those who are mathematically challenged that is over 100 mpg in a 4 cylinder vehicle and represents the potential savings of trillions of barrels of oil and billions of tons of carbon emissions – this primary source of global warming.

What ever happened to the Pough carburetor? Like all great Western inventions—if they don't serve the special interest of the wealthy corporate owners—the patents are bought and suppressed. If the inventor refuses to sell, hired goons put them permanently out of business, if you know what I mean. If you stop and think about the actual implications of this you will either swoon or feel like hurting somebody. Now the polar caps are melting, the earth is imbalanced, and huge climatic maelstroms are on man's horizon. But, that is not the worst of it. Fossil fuels are not renewable and their cost is subject to supply and demand. Wealthier nations suppress the development of poorer nations by hogging the supply and keeping the prices high. Conservation is not in the best interests of corporate capitalism. Now,

I'm neither an economist nor a nation maker, but common sense says having an energy dependency on a source that is neither renewable nor sustainable is a formula for disaster!

India is a great country with a proven track record for excellence. Not only is it able to keep astride the G8's, it has the potential to leave them behind. Admittedly, there are more engineers here than Bajajs. If you're capable of putting satellites in orbit and missiles in your neighbors' front doors—tell me—why not build a better mouse trap? Why do you insist on following the lead of other nations? Have you ever wondered why God has given you the wings of imagination? Don't be afraid to spread them and soar!

Not only does India have the potential to invent alternative energy devices like the world has never seen before, but what really gives you a leg up is the fact you are the oldest nation with a continuous history. In the course of eons you evolved philosophy to its zenith. People come from around the world to study it. I keep repeating the principle of *dharma* will not only put you to the head of class—you will teach the other nations its meaning. Many of you haven't a clue as to what I am talking about and think I'm merely stroking your ego. Some of you understand the relationship between *dharma* and *karma*. When humans live *adharmically* the *karma* they create is negative. How that impacts your home, village, town, city, state, country, and planet depends on the magnitude of the action. The West has a much different concept of *dharma* – self service – a social value many of you are quickly emulating!

Like you I find myself asking: *What can we do about changing anything in the world?* Plenty. First, support legislation for alternative energy by encouraging your leadership. Ask your representatives to allocate research funds and earmark them for the IT colleges. Encourage young minds to create. The professor and family I stay with in the Bangalore area has an older model scooter and makes do. I left behind a sports car, Jeep Grand Cherokee, and pickup truck—all these were for my personal use and I took them for granted. And, of course my wife had her own little car! The world wants—and deserves—the things I grew up with and walked away from. So, have at it *Bharat*. In the meanwhile, with sea levels expected to rise 13 meters in parts of the world now might be a good time to consider purchasing some rural land—say around Hyderabad. In a few years it may be worth a fortune when it becomes ocean-front property!

❧❧

Wave of the Future
The Push for Accelerated Development

Did you know I'm a Scorpio?—not just a single but a double! With Pluto in the mid-heaven it makes me very psychic. Lately, I've been having such a haunting vision I was considering visiting an exorcist! I see a bright and shiny future for India. I see a phenomenal increase in national productivity and each individual's personal fortune. And— I also see how the change is going to come about.

Statistical studies from the last global census shows that 15 percent of the world's population of 6 billion live in 22 countries known collectively as the *developed nations*. The rest of the 4.5 billion live in the *developing nations*. The average annual income of a middle-class worker in the developed nations is $25,000 versus $5,000 in the developing nation. This huge disparity in income is one of the great lures attracting foreign workers to immigrate to the more prosperous countries. Often this proves to be an illusion as I have seen in the case of migrant workers from Mexico—who enjoy an income of about $10,000. They steal across the border only to find that the reality of living in a developed nation is harsh—as income is in proportion to the cost of living. Most come seeking the Great Payday then experience a hellish living condition, being forced to the bottom of the barrel, not being able to find sustainable work, sacrificing their country, culture, and family ties. Many get caught in the undertow of Western vice, falling into the toilets of drugs, prostitution, and organized crime.

In the developed nations you find a tremendous amount of industrialization. Machines are used for everything—to monitor your children in another room, to automatically open doors and turn on lights in your house—my mother owns a *Roomba*—a saucer shaped robotic that automatically vacuums her carpeted house. In the developing nations much of the industrial activity is done by hand. In printing shops you'll find guys hand stamping numbers or logos on receipt books, guys in elevators whose job it is to press the button of your destination floor—they're repaving a road in front of my house and have been for six months and still have six months to go—all by hand. But, by far the greatest employer of human time and energy is agriculture.

Last year, celebrating my wife's citizenship and a conference I was attending in Chicago, we drove across the Northern United States. Leaving Yellowstone National Park—a monument of natural beauty and abundant wildlife—we headed across the Plains States. For two days as far as the eye could see to the horizon was a vast sea of soybeans and cornstalks. What struck me as odd, even eerie, was the absence of humans. Where was everybody? Who kept an eye on things? Then, once in a while you would see a huge mechanical device mowing through the amber grain, leaving a two-lane wide swatch in the head-high fields. Only 5 percent of the workforce is devoted to agriculture in the developed nations. Guess what the number is in the developing nations?

Depends where you are, but on average between 50-65 percent! It's a whooping number. If we use the lower figure, in India, we're talking half a billion people deriving their incomes from agricultural work. Now, here is the big dilemma—if you mechanize Ag what are you going to do with the 45 percent of displaced workers? The nation would collapse. China faces a similar problem. I like quoting Gandhi—and occasionally I actually come close to quoting him correctly! He said, "*The heart and soul of India is her villages.*" But, the modern world is knocking at your door. Most people—even villagers—want all those gadgets that their Western cousins have—like 42 inch plasma televisions with satellite link, digital cameras, popcorn makers and electric can openers. You yuppies want cars with personal GPS and OnStar systems. Locked your keys in the car? Call the toll free number and within minutes the GPS locates the car and unlocks it. Can't find your favorite restaurant? Push a button on the rearview mirror and you're linked to an information command center. You never have to fear about the vehicle being stolen because the GPS is built in. It's cool. But, technology costs bucks. Where's the money going to come from?

Since I was young I've had psychic ability. I see India slowly waking up to the fact that she is quite capable of competing with the Big Boys. I see her shifting some of her intelligencia from mindless follow-the-leader copy-cat college degrees and creating some liberal curriculums that reward risk-taking and stimulate genius. Maybe a few think tanks to pool your best minds. I see her creating a large network of trade schools where young men and women from the villages can go to receive technical training in manufacturing and construction – nation building. The developed nations seldom import skilled labor—they form trade unions and train their workers. A carpenter in California is paid more than a doctor in Delhi. What's wrong with this picture? I see a huge force of educated, skilled workers building this country's infrastructure—not at the slowpoke speed you see government projects snailing along—but with *Power*. I see young men and women excited about going to college—not to study point & click computer engineering, but civil engineering, construction and industrial management, urban development and planning. I see waves of Westerners flocking to India to purchase billions of dollars in manufactured goods and professional services – electric cars, energy devices, healthcare, pharmaceuticals, computers, hardware, software, underwear, textiles, text books, hand craft, space craft. My dream is limited – may yours have wings. I see your booming future evolving from the fruiting seeds of your past. Then I snapped out of my revere and see the bullock cart crawling down the torn up road in front of my house and ask: *Is this a vision or my overactive imagination*?!?

࿔

Maps & Territories
Abdul Kalam's Vision: A Response

After swimming in the ocean in the little fishing village south of Rameshwaram, to the astonishment and delight of the locals, our rickshaw driver took my wife and I by your family home and we had the pleasure of meeting your charming elder brother. Not long after, a copy of *Wings Of Fire* came to my hand and I was greatly impressed by your character, commitment, and accomplishment. Not truly responsible for the gifts God bestows upon us, from somewhere in my being a musical composition took birth, *Bharat I Believe*.

Subsequently, after a stint in the States and a whirl through Argentina and Chile, I found myself back in India. I had heard about *Vision 2020*, a road map that leads India to the status of a fully developed nation in the leap of one generation, but the book vendor at the Leela Palace was out of stock. However, he had *Ignited Minds*, a 2020 summary with an inspirational message to the youth of your nation. Immediately, I found applications for the book. A doctor friend at an ultra modern hospital made a comment to his staff, something to the effect that white Westerners are superior. I took the remark as solicitatious. Armed with *Ignited Minds,* on my next visit, quoted: "The quality of the Indian mind is equal to the quality of …the Anglo mind… I think we have developed an inferiority complex…" and admonished him and the staff to reform their diminutive thinking.

To paraphrase the gist of your message you have defined five areas you would like to see rapidly developed—education in a vast network so that every citizen can know the joys of reading, writing and accessing information; national health care; agriculture;

information and communication (IT); infrastructure and critical technology. You underscore these developments by the cultivation of human values and the sustenance of faith in God irregardless of religious denomination, saying, "The stronger the spiritual wealth the stronger will become all other forms of wealth".

President Kalam, you certainly have unequivocal faith in your country, and have demonstrated faith is reciprocal—not blind nor misplaced. *Rohini* is such an incredible story. I narrate it often, reminding the citizens of India that they should take pride and be bolstered by that national accomplishment—putting a satellite into obit as oxen pulled plows through flooded rice fields. You have seen the results of coordinated effort in the mission mood and speak from experience. Sir, you see developed India as a network of industrious and economically connected villages, not the centralization of city commerce, served by the new sciences of telemedicine, tele-education and e-commerce. One of the things that raises my brow is your exploding population. A successful business woman, Tej Kaul, once told me, "Making babies is something Indians are very good at." Here comes the rub. Mechanized agriculture, in the developed nations currently employs 5% of the workforce. President Kalam, if India were to mechanize agriculture what do you propose doing with about 550 million displaced workers? [Figures based on your 61% estimate.] We know from history that hungry unemployed people revolt against their government.

You surprised me with the statistic that India is the largest dairy producer in the world. And, of course, my capitalistic mind *ka-chinged* the cash register. Export! Not milk but cheese. Having traveled extensively through India, *paneer* is ubiquitous, called same in Uttar Pradesh as in Kerala. Europeans laugh at Americans—we produce very few varieties of cheese—mostly yellow and white, cheddar and jack. But, we import tons of it from Europe. Visit any upscale grocer in the Bangalore footprint and you will find Gouda, Blue, and

Parmesan cheeses as well as other varieties—excellent quality—not imported from France or Italy but from Pondicherry, Tamil Nadu. Sold anywhere from $12-30 per pound abroad, there is an untapped potential in export trade and the creation of a cheese industry. How much does India get for one ton—2,000 pounds—of iron ore? Think: *Dairy gold*.

I almost fell out of my chair with excitement – which probably would have created a ripple affect among the fellow airline passengers – when I read about telemedicine. India has the potential of becoming a major player in health care – a multibillion dollar industry in the West. When American drug companies wanted $10,000 per person for HIV meds for a large project President Clinton was sponsoring in China, he purchased them in India at a tenth of the cost. At the risk of sounding redundant I'll repeat—many citizens here know the meaning of *dharma*. When *dava* and *dharma* connect, when this country shoulders the role of healing those who hurt and providing health services at a modest to moderate cost, the rest of the ailing world will beat a path to your doorstep, as many of us already do. President Kalam, with the emerging IT India wants to take the initiative to forge ahead and develop this new field. The IT and medical communities want to integrate their specialized knowledge, and produce *internationally patented software in telemedicine*. There is a beautiful patent office in Chennai, just waiting for work! I don't think you emphasized this point strongly enough. ***Patented technology will help concretize your vision.*** You don't want to fall back in this race or wait to see how other nations are progressing. Because if you do, India, as you poignantly state, "will continue being a cheap labor source for the wealthy industrial nations". Jump on it; involve the government. The stakes are too high.

India is also in a key position to score big points in the match against the West in the area of bio-science and technology. Perhaps the formation of an Asian Alliance with your neighbors may work to your advantage. Thanks to President Bush, who voted against Congress funding research in the great new medical field of stem cells, other nations are fast tracking their research and development and pulling ahead in this vital race. Small countries like Singapore are getting into the act and patenting their discoveries. My state, California, saw how important this science is and last November the voters appropriated $3 billion for research. If my readers haven't heard or have forgotten, during the embryonic stage of human development from neutral *stem cells* the body manufactures about 100 different specialized cells that form all its components. By isolating and injecting stem cells into diseased areas of the body, they multiply and replace damaged cells. People with heart conditions, blindness, nerve and brain damage such as Alzheimer's, and other organs or tissues can be repaired. Herald as **the most important discovery in medicine ever made**, it has the potential of curing all non-viral diseases. President Bush will be happy to hear California is aggressively searching for stem cells to cure *stupid*.

Of course, the area of interest that lifts me off the launch pad is alternative energy. India doesn't want to be last in line or having to buy User's Licensing from nations holding the patents on nanotechnology. India wants to get a good kick off the starting block. You should be not only in this race, but out front.

With your industrial strength, with Tata, Bajaj, and Leyland-Ashok why on earth aren't you world leaders in electric vehicles? Remember how the Japanese shocked Detroit with 4-cylinder cars? Everybody wants them – but Detroit won't let us have them. Now that global warming is out of the closet and the oil barons, who successfully lobbied against energy saving technology are loosing their strangle hold on consumers, EV's will reincarnate. We should all demand an arrest warrant for the criminal corporate officers who killed the electric car. Most people are unaware that about 50% of early American cars were electric. People loved them; you could charge

87

them at home, and they only cost a fraction of what a gallon of gasoline costs. But, then, look at who makes America's energy policies!

Sir, did you hear we are generating electricity from permanent magnets and hydrogravidic devices? It can't get any simpler than this. As I told Professor J.N. Sinha, Dean, Dept of Engineering and Applied Technology, Banares Hindu University, "If our cave dwelling ancestors could produce fire by striking flints and rubbing sticks, surely modern man can generate a few electrons as simply."

On behalf of the 'little guys' in the world – most of us – it seems to me the leaders of all nations would be prioritizing desalinization research and development. The science community is telling us that the fresh water pack is melting at about ten million square acres per year. And, the melting is accelerating. I'm not a rocket scientist – but even a shade tree carpenter can tell you that when the snow pack melts and the rivers run dry terrestrial life will suffer. I'm sure your science advisors have informed you that the damaged thermohaline may actually cause the oceanic conveyor to stop. And when the nutrients that upwell in the conveyor cease to feed the plankton, the first link of the food chain, we are facing a potential mass die-off of planetary life unlike any other since the Permian Extinction. No water on land; no current flowing in the sea is a formula for disaster. Stem cells, space exploration, EV's, vacations to Aruba, Visa and MasterCard have no value when the well literally runs dry! Desalinization, in addition to bore welling the aquifer, may be what keeps the human species from becoming a rememberant in the fossil record. When Washington D.C. keeps politicizing science, kissing lobbyist's butts, while pumping $455 billion a year into national defense (2005 budget, which does not include Afghanistan and Iraq – a defense spending greater than the sum total of all the other nations) – it becomes the duty of those nations upholding *dharma* to come forward and take the lead. A new world is in the making. Unfortunately, many will suffer as the dross is burned off in the crucible of transformation. President Kalam, what is India doing to prepare for the consequence of global warming? Water will be the currency of the future. Do you not see this?

President Kalam you say, "Poverty is India's greatest enemy…" With all due respect, sir, I would like to suggest that to measure India's wealth by foreign economic standards may be doing the people of your great nation an undeserved injustice. India has bought into the Western paradigm where everything is equated and quantified by material possessions and bank account bottom lines. I see it everywhere I go – measuring Eastern standards by Western values. Sir, will you not give a few score points for how healthy and vital your countrymen are? Will you not increase India's score card for having tight knit families and societal units? Is it fair to foist Western obsessions on your countrymen? Does everybody need a Roomba, remote, I-Pod and plasma to be 'developed'? If so, Vision 2020 needs corrective lenses. One year, while meditating in a large *mandir*, I was roused by the unmistakable smell of cow dung—earthy, organic, not unpleasant. I opened my eyes and sitting on the black granite floor in front of me were three farmers from nearby Andra fields. Unshaven, in soiled *dhotis*, browned by the sun, muscular, good looking, and vivacious. Probably between the three they didn't have a hundred rupees. Still, Life surged in these men who I'll never forget. Visit their village and you will find it much cleaner than overcrowded cities. Rustic, picturesque, the people are engaged, employed, well fed, socially connected homeowners. Yes, they may not have a world overview, an ATM card, or lack the secular knowledge many seem to value—but they have something their critics don't—practical skills, common sense, and a certain innocence money cannot buy but only tends to corrupt. With all due respect, sir, to call them poor insults their dignity.

Mister President, your vision for India's prosperous future is exciting and stimulates our thinking. But, there are maps and territories—drawing boards and launch pads. Huge undertakings challenge humans to exhibit their greatness. Shifting from an agrarian to industrial nation may result by developing the nation along the highways and byways you have defined. Finding the key to unlock the economy and its inherent abundance is imperative – but, abundance with responsibility, not an orgy of objects. There is a wealth in India that cannot be measured in monetary terms—a unique watermark embedded in its culture. Is the Western paradigm truly the best model? Why then did Gandhi retreat to the land and emulate his agrarian ancestors? Perhaps, like a block of stone, India's 21st Century world image is still in the Carver's mind, being revealed chip after chip, meticulous and flawless. Men of faith who have glimpsed His glory patiently await the unveiling.

Made in India
Comparing Corporate Paradigms

Watermelon pink Margaritas – neon green frozen Daiquiris; animated conversation, silverware chiming against heavy plates, background din at a high decibel – the sound of a successful restaurant. The waitress arrived with a plastic laminated menu, both photos and descriptions, which I perused page after page. *Chicken Fajita, Texas-style Ribs, Cajun Catfish, New York Sirloin.* Almost out of embarrassment I asked if they had any non-meat choices and she hooked me up with a cheese pizza,. The red and white awning, the *art deco* wall mounts, as if the designer had empted a sea captain's cabin, was all too familiar. And the logo, TGIF, distinctly American. Location: downtown Bangalore. Then I got to thinking, *Indians don't thank God it's Friday – they thank God it's Saturday!* What's up?

In the courtyard, rent-a-cops were cleaning up glass shards. Some vandal had throw a brick through the plate glass window. *Odd*, I thought. *You don't see a lot of senseless property destruction in India like you do in America.* Then I noticed the guard shack was located right next to a liquor store – a typical 10' x 12' concrete stall, with shelves stocked full of Johnny Walker Red Label, Jack Daniels, and Wild Turkey – Tennessee and Kentucky bourbon –'Sippin' whiskey'. The puzzle pieces were slowly starting to come together. *Damn! Corporate America is really into you guys*, I thought.

Feeling depressed I trudged home to my flat in Rastum Baugh, by-passed the elevator preferring the staircase, bolted my door, crack open a bottle of chilled *cocojal*, kicked back on the sofa, and surfed the dishnet. Not having watched television in India, I was blown away at the advertising. American Express, Quaker Oats, Colgate toothpaste, Miranda Sorbet, Smirnoff vodka, Pedigree Dog Food, Frito Lay, Nestle, Orbit gum, Kellogg's – it went on and on. *They're into you worst than I thought.*

American corporations are shaping India's image. And here's where it gets tricky. We are two different cultures with different philosophies and evolutionary patterns. The East has thousands of years of continued history in commerce, trading domestically and internationally, using the concepts of *karma* and *dharma*. How many times have I seen a merchant close a transaction, thanking God and pressing the currency to his forehead? I can not recall one business or house I've ever visited in India that didn't have at least one faith icon. *Ever!* In the Eastern business model morality, ethics and faith are components. In the Western corporate paradigm Profit is the God worshipped; the generals of industry will mobilize the country's war machine to protect its sacred cow; the only rule of the game is to win – at all cost. And, as global warming becomes a part of your personal experience, you may wonder how mankind ever allowed such a inequitable system to originate.

In the late 1890's, attorneys citing the 14th amendment – a law created to protect the rights of newly unchained slaves – succeeded in convincing the courts to issue the first corporate charter, giving birth to the behemoth company, Standard Oil. A *business entity*, the corporation has all the power to act as a human, however, unlike a human it is not required to exhibit love, compassion, fairness, logic – it's sole purpose is to make money– and unlike a human, it never dies. Today we see the consequence of this business model and the monsters it creates – leaders of powerful nations invading weaker countries to protect their corporate interests; the suppression of technologies good for us and the environment in order to protect the profits of a few share holders who enjoy a phenomenal economic disparity.

Last year I visited Argentina and Chile, both beautiful developing countries with delicate economies; Argentina's collapsed in 2003. Because of proximity they do a lot of business with the United States. In the seaport Valdiva, I had a sudden rude awakening. Inside a supermarket, walking down an aisle, I found myself surrounded by American products – many of the brands listed above. *This is bad,* I thought, *Chile is agriculturally rich. Why import food?* It got worst. At the checkout I was shocked by the prices. Groceries were more expensive than in America! Consumers were being victimized by predacious corporate retailing. The same held true for Argentina.

Don't take me wrong, I love my country; we are a nation of hardworking people, Monday thru Friday, 9 - 5, struggling to achieve or maintain the American Dream. We are like cosmic kids always curious, which prompts us to research and explore. And, most of us would not want to risk eating food acquired by unholy means or sleeping under a roof that was built with bad money. However, the Western corporate paradigm is long overdue for an extensive remodel by nation builders.

India has great products and certainly can feed her own people. Who needs Quaker Oats? Grow some oats in a field next to the rice, harvest it, roll the oats, put them in a box that has the primary colors red, yellow, blue – call it *Whitefield Grains* – put a picture of a guy that looks like Prime Minister Manmohan Singh in a cameo in the corner of the box, and sell it for less money than the import. Like soda pop? Water, sugar, sodium bicarbonate – oops, almost forgot – spiked with addictive caffeine – are the base; add lime oil and you've got Sprite. Add orange oil and you've got Fanta. Add cola syrup and you've got Coke's Indian subsidiary, ThumbsUp, which has got so much caffeine my *jata* stands on end! Commercial: Two macho young dudes with 3 day breads dressed in Banana Republic garb – cobra catchers – on the precipice of a snake pit in a sugar cane field. From their soiled field packs they crack out ice cold bottles of *Deva's Jaggery*

Dew – camera pans for a close-up as the sweaty guys guzzle refreshment – then simultaneously leap into the pit. CUT! Toothpaste? The sales are in the billions. Flavors: *elaichi, mint, rose, dalchini, saunf* – maybe *lal mirchi* for our friends in South India! Commercial: Boy and girl with great physical chemistry, getting close up and personal. Get the picture?

American marketing is bringing us closer together, creating in you the same desire that we are all indoctrinated with – purchasing corporate products that are over-sugared, over salted, high in fat and cholesterol, overpriced and often produced at the misery of others and high cost to the environment. Staring blankly into the blue TV screen, consumers are subliminally brainwashed. Is there a choice?

Once we know the secret of the magician tricks they no longer fascinate. There's power in knowledge. When you know you're being victimized you can reverse the process; you have the power to say, no. That is what the Mute button is for. "No, thanks Tropicana, make mine a Kerala *cocojal*." Consumers are powerful. India's history was changed forever by consumers when, spearheaded by Mahatma Gandhi, the citizens collectively boycotted salt. This simple coordinated act was the kinesis that toppled the British Empire's reign.

International trade, in theory, is good for us all, stimulating the economy of both the producing and consuming nation – encouraging competition, often bringing superior quality goods and services to the market at the lowest prices, and offering consumers products not found in their native lands. However, when we become dependant on the products of foreign nations, we surrender our own production power and are at their mercy. And when the companies are lacking moral principles, *dharma,* that subjugation comes at a high price. It hurts to see India loosing her virginity, getting screwed by the Western moguls of marketing. Sometimes the best defense is a strong offensive. Government should encourage and increase the number of small regional businesses who can manufacture comparative consumer goods without the high overhead costs of shipping, distribution and advertising. Government is capable of offering low interest loans and special incentives, such as preferential consideration for women and disadvantaged citizens bidding on government work. What I found useful and took advantage of was free consultations with retired business professionals, who can double check your business plan, help solve problems and provide mentoring. Government should create, if it hasn't already, a Small Business Administration. The ultimate weapon is consumer choice freed from the mental muscle of marketing.

The absence of domestically produced consumer goods allows foreign manufactures to flood the market with their own products. Recently, I went shopping for a laptop computer – the old Toshiba had a *Pentium arrest*. Wanting to support these articles by putting my money where my mouth is, I went looking for a computer with the logo Made In India. After a week of traveling from one end of town to the other, I was in for a rather rude awakening. India doesn't manufacture a computer – a country that graduates three times more IT engineers per capita than the rest of the world! Go figure?! But, it comes close – H.C.L. and Wipro assemble parts from abroad to make a generic product; Acer manufactures in Malaysia and markets in India.

The logo Made In India should attract you, instill pride, and be synonymous with quality. Before Japan perfected manufacturing the country flooded America with cheap imitation goods. They were master copycats. However, the quality was lacking and Made In Japan was synonymous with *cheap*. There was a learning curve. Today look at how successful they've become. Team work, national pride, ingenuity, a strong cohesive government puts Japan at the top of the food chain. In his vision for India's rapid development President Kalam sees manufacturing and marketing in the private business sector and 'selling' the country's national image as imperative. Perhaps in the not to distant future, when you've perfected both sectors, American youngster will be pestering their mothers for a bottle of *Deva's Jaggery Dew*.

Community Service
A Target Rich Environment

The classroom was a stifling oven and a strong smell of kerosene filled the air. A match could have created an explosion. 50 little tykes crammed in one classroom and 40 in another. By the day's end I had given written notice to the owner of the school property informing him of the leaking gas and the potential liability for *child endangerment*, and had drafted an electrical plan which I submitted to the executive administrator, who runs several schools and various other programs for the economically disadvantaged and educationally underprivileged—India's poor. Within the day the gas leak was corrected. Within a month the school was wired with electricity, plugs, switches and ceiling fans; the classrooms painted inside and out; all the building repairs had been completed. And, at this writing—the children are awaiting their new playground. No—I am not affiliated with any organization, nor had I any ulterior motives or vested interest in the property. For me I saw a *scoring opportunity in a target rich environment* and a way to constructively use surplus wealth. Easy-peasy.

It doesn't matter whether you're a theist or an atheist—what matters is how you interact with people and the society you live in. Each one of us has some concept of who we are at a level deeper than our 'name and frame', and what we can do to further our personal development. Living in India has helped me evolve my own humanity or spirituality much more than was possible in America for two reasons. First there is no dearth of need; on every street in every city, town or village you will find people underserved. It is no wonder

Mother Teresa choose this place to demonstrate to the world the meaning of Lord Jesus' teaching, which is paraphrased as: *Hands that help are holier than lips that pray.* Secondly, there is a disparity between our economies; my cost of living is almost 10 times higher in the United States; here I find that my limited income actually puts me in another tax bracket! What to do with all those extra rupees at the end of the month? Simple—earmark them for service projects.

At home in California I'm involved with many continuing projects. Even there you'll find an indigent population; whites who have lost their lives to the ravages of drugs and alcohol, blacks who have likewise back-slid mostly through limited education and employment opportunities, and migrant Hispanics who illegally enter the States then can't find work. Several of our projects involve feeding homeless people. We prepare bag lunches for two different populations—our families purchase groceries and get together to make the lunches, then take them to a distribution point. One group of friends adopted a mother and her 8 kids. We help them with food and supplies; I was able to hook them up with a refrigerator, washing machine and dryer. Another group I participate with feeds a delicious hot dinner once a month at a shelter that houses about 100 homeless. Another small group receives money through private and church donations—although not affiliated with a church, temple, mosque, or synagogue. We meet once a month at a wholesale market and purchase 5,000 lbs. (2,300 kilos) of rice and beans, which we parcel into 2.5 and 5 kilo bags. Later, we load the parcels into a large truck that drives to a camp of migrant farm workers where the food is distributed. Once, we were informed teenage girls would not wear some beautiful donated dresses. Why? Because they felt ashamed that their underwear was old and worn. It grated the core of human dignity. Our little group organized a community drive to collect brand new underwear for boys and girls of all sizes and ages. The response was overwhelming and the community gave hundreds of pairs.

You probably didn't hear about this, but two years ago a group of my friends from India living in the Silicon Valley area did a project I participated in. We rented a huge shipping container and conducted a mass community drive, extending over a hundred miles, collecting Indian and general clothing, toys, school supplies, household items— and, wait until you hear this—the first five feet, about 9 cubic yards, was all medical supplies – heart catheters, OT plastics, medicines, etc. – donated by a large hospital! The container was packed with 1,008 boxes, uniformly numbered and labeled for Customs, shipped to Chennai, then transported to Hyderabad, where the contents were unloaded and distributed to poor families through a volunteer network. The medical supplies were donated to a hospital that serves the poor. I experienced a *leela* which I talk about in *Miracles In America*. I worked with the same IT group as a Spanish translator doing *grama seva* where we held a medical camp and provided ten kilo 'care packages' to migrant farm labors, pockets of poverty in the US.

Our friend doctor Nilima Sabharwal started Home of Hope, www.hohinc.org, eight years ago with one home for orphans near Chennai—today she has about 1,500 kids in 12 different venues spread across India, supported mostly by expatriates. Home of Hope provides housing, education, health care and mentoring, and needs all the help it can get. I can tell you more—our friend Princess Funmi Bodunde, using her influential position, was able to get the Nigerian government to commit $110 million dollars to construct a postgrad medical campus in Kaduna? How about our friends, the Rotary Club in Bangalore, who purchased and constructed a hospice in Whitefield? A friend of mine volunteers her time there. Have a family member or know someone who has a heart condition? O.P. Khanna is waiting to welcome them at the Manipal Heart Foundation. I am blessed in my service network.

Give a man a fish and he'll feed his family today; teach a man to fish and he'll feed his family for life. It is far better to give people a *hand up* rather than a *handout.* Education is the key. For the poor it can be learning some job skill or a *micro-loan.* Billionaire George Sorros set up a general fund that caters mostly to women in developing nations. The micro-loans are about $250 max, and give the gals an opportunity to start a business. I love the example of the lady in Bangladesh who bought a cell phone and block of airtime with her loan. Not only was it the first cell phone but *the only phone* in her village. She made enough profit that not only did she quickly repay her loan, but she was able to send her daughter to college! Knowledge is power.

Service opportunities are unlimited. But, there are a few things we should keep in mind. Lord Jesus talked about serving in a *filial* manner—seeing the person you serve as a member of your own human family. India's internationally acclaimed spiritual teacher, Sai Baba, says: *Forget the good you do others; remember the good others do you.* When we remember the good others do us we are instilled with humility; when we think of the good we do others it breeds pride and limits our ability to do more service. Makes goods sense. Personally, I see service as a way of connecting with others and elevating my own humanity. I become more loving, caring, and score a lot of points with my mother who brags to all her friends what a good guy I am! When you love what you are doing the obstacles are nothing more than challenges to apply your ability to resolve them.

This country has taught me more about service than any other teacher. And I'm constantly on the lookout for *seva* opportunities. Currently, I've got my eyes on a community at the end of the block where people live in huts constructed by bending saplings, then covering the framework with palm leaves and blue plastic tarps. No water, toilets or electricity. Dirt floors, open fire pits, bare bones. Maybe I'll send over a case or two of microwavable popcorn and some Coca-Cola!

᪐᪐

A Letter Home
Part 2

Dear Brother: I am once again in India and you will be glad to hear not much has changed—only my perspective. It is probably just as well that you didn't come as the frustration of living here might prove too great a challenge. Even simple things like putting postage on a letter can try one's patience—gluing the envelope, sealing it, gluing the stamp, and while waiting for it to dry, cleaning the excess glue off your hands and clothes—then finding somewhere to mail the letter. As our system of postal delivery is not here, and there are no corner boxes, it's challenging. But the fact I am sending this letter shows that I care and am prepared to make sacrifices for you. I know how easily you unravel, so it's probably best you stayed home—I'd hate to see your circuits overloaded.

Father will flip when he hears that I've turned native—Indian American —not just a little but whole hog—braided hair *jata*, *rudraksha mala* beads, *dhoti* and sandals, down to the sandalwood *tilak* and patchouli oil. By accident or providence, I stumbled upon the ancient *vedic* culture while traveling with monks in the Himalays (a tall range of mountains in the northern part of the continent, in case you've forgotten your geography). Most Indians don't know about this aspect of their own culture, so busy are they running after things Western. Father would think it's a colossal waste of time that could be more effectively used doing business. You know how he loves to make money "the old fashion way"—ripping off natural resources, exploiting cheap labor, price gouging on exports and undercutting imports. He'd hate that I've been wasting my money, actually throwing it away, supplying schools with basic tools. He'd think I was helping the competition get ahead and would not at all approve.

Also, during one spell of madness, I arranged to have photographs taken of all the children at a school and a group shot of each class— a pretty neat trick for someone who doesn't even own a camera—and an example of how clever Americans are. While prepping the kids for their photos I noticed one shy girl around fourteen who, as I discovered upon close contact, had a defect. Unlike yours, which is mental—hers was physical. Also, unlike yours hers was not congenital nor elective, but a result of an illness that depleted her vitamin A. For five rupees (no, bro—these are not red semi-precious stones, but Indian currency worth about twenty cents) the vitamins could have been replaced and her vision spared. The girl was not only blind, but the discolored eye protruded disfiguring the poor child. She also had terrible teeth. Don't let Father know what I'm about to tell you. He'd come unglued. I don't know what came over me, but suddenly I felt this strong attraction—like this girl was my daughter. The urge to help not subject to debate or cross examination—was imperative. I could not believe how brave the girl was; like a trooper going off to war, facing the frightening ordeal without flinching. I know how squeamish you are so I will spare you the graphic details. With a minimum amount of effort and a ridiculously small sum of dollars, considering the stakes, I was able to sponsor her surgery and orthodonistry. Her mother asked if I would also help the girl's sister, whose dental nightmare required surgery; I said, "Sure. Why not?" Hush up about this. Father would never understand. He thinks his kids are the only kids worth investing in. After all, blood is thicker than water. If I told him all humans have blood, I'm not sure if he'd think I was using logic as a tool to imply that all people are family, therefore worth investing in. Not a word of this or you'll be needing some surgery when I come home!

Currently I'm traveling with monks through the Deccan, a large land area up north. We have only the bare minimum requirements, which don't include pizza and Pepsi-Cola. We don't bath with soap, which I'm sure you'd find appealing, even though we do dip a lot in an ice cold river called the Ganga. Dipping is supposed to be good for your soul, but I haven't figured out how that part works. We spend a lot of time mornings and evenings warming up with buffalo chip. (I know what you're thinking. No, bro, we're not burning barbeque flavored potato chips—but making cow dung fires.) We eat with our hands off plates made from tree leafs stitched together. Knowing how much you used to love to play with your food you'd probably enjoy eating with us, even though you wouldn't care for the simple food and the total lack of any meat. Our guru, the head honcho here, is very cool. He never combs or cuts his hair, sits most of the day with his legs crossed meditating—no—I'm sorry, bro—the word does sound a lot like 'medicating', but has nothing to do with drugs. Father would find sitting quietly without thoughts a torture; for him 'time is money'. (He may not waste much time but it seems to me he wastes most of his money investing in things that only bring him happiness for short periods.)

After so many months of living like this, strange things are starting to happen to me. Some of the monks say they see energy, like a halo around me. I can not say what I have not seen. But, one thing is certain—a feeling of oneness is starting to engulf me. All the toys I left at home have lost their power to attract me. (If you want you can have my model electrical coils, generators and inverters. Just make sure you're grounded before plugging anything in. Okay?) My compass needle is pointing north. I will return to the mountains and learn the meaning of a few new words. As you can see by this letter, I use far too many already. If I can only learn the meaning of *prema, sathya, dharma, shanti and ahimsa* I feel I could give up speech all together.

I promised in my last letter in 2005 to bring you here. And, I will someday when you are prepared to come, when you can be away from home without your Game Boy and remote control, when you can go for long intervals without eating, endure hot weather, and aren't overwhelmed by poverty and poor sanitary conditions. Otherwise, if I brought you today, you'd be like a heron who's caught a snake too large to swallow but won't let go—both suffer—you being here; India, having you here.

Postscript

Returning to Bangalore in 2007, one and a half years after most of these articles were written, I was in for a shock. I rubbed my eyes to make sure I was in the right city and not in Singapore by some twist of fate. It had radically transformed. Traffic moved smoothly; the air quality had greatly improved, I couldn't find a single cow wandering about—I had to go up North to Varanasi where large city herds still roam freely—and, wonder of wonders, after six years of construction the Rustam Baugh overpass is nearing completion as a new modern monorail breaks ground. Search though I may, not one wall pisser. Shucks! I'd have to write an apology. No – better make it a retraction! Yet, I wondered how so much change was possible and concluded these articles must have been circulated amongst the leadership! What else could it be?!?

I hope you enjoyed ramblings with me as I rambled about *sona ki chiriya,* and found in these letters both entertainment and food for thought. Being a *saddhu* myself – okay!...with a lot of disposable income – I'm searching for answers to Life's deepest questions. As oil is found in Arabia, diamonds in South Africa, holy people are India's abundant treasure. This land is replete with saints, sages, seers and savants, sworn to serve humanity. The message of Gurudev, an echo of the Vedas, entreats people of *Bharat* to seek the truth and live *dharmically.* Is there any better message?

Also, you'll be pleased to hear I am no longer fixing India, but simply experiencing her. While walking through a hot, congested area up north, bombarded by bad smells, unpaved trafficked roads, people throwing trash on the streets, animals and biological waste everywhere, flies buzzing the uncovered food vended by the multitude lining the potholed thoroughfare, I thought to myself, *When I'm in America – I miss this way of life.* What a strange notion. But, it came with understanding. Rural India is part of my own human history. These rustic folks show me where I've come from – a hereditary past long forgotten. And, although they do not realize – I must seem so awkward to them, overdressed, too clean, too *gori*, too *videsh* – still, I represent where their children are going, economically as East and West continue their interesting courtship.

My travels carried me far; still, I'm left with two nagging questions. Having 'dipped' in the Ganga at Varanasi, the Gangotri at Allahabad, the river head at Badrinath high in the Himalayas, and had my 22 *tirthams* at Rameswaram, I want to know: "Is it the dip that makes us holy? Or, the purified heart?" The second question also baffles the daylights out of me. When you pilgrimage to Tirupati and stand before the *murthi* of Venkateshwara, Balaji, there is no denying the powerful energy that emanates from the veiled Lord. For centuries the people of *Bharat* have been repaying Lord Kubera for a loan so Srinivas could wed the beautiful Padmavati. What puzzles me is three-fold: "How much did Srinivas actually borrow from Lord Kubera? Secondly, "How many more years are left until the loan is paid off?" And, "Is the Bank of Hyderabad giving India the best interest rate?"

|| hari om namah shivaya ||

Glossary

Acharya: spiritual teacher

Adharma: unrighteous, against dharma

Agrabati: incense

Ahimsa: non-violent thoughts, words and actions

Arati: ritualistic offering of light; symbolizing illumination of the darkened mind

Arjuna: warrior king and mighty bowman from the epic Mahabharata

Asatoma sadgamaya: "from untruth lead us to truth...", Upanishadic Mantra

Bajaj: vehicle manufacture

Bala: child, young

Bharat: India's ancient name; 'land of god'

Bharatiya sanskriti: the ancient culture of Bharat

Chai: black, sweetened milk tea

Chapati: flat staple pan bread

Chappels: sandals

Chaykada: variety of black tea

Choli: female blouse worn under a sari

Chudi dhar: lady's fashionable dress

Chuni: lady's shawl covering the bosom

Cocojal: milk from green coconut

Dakshina: alms given to a holy person; bribe

Dalchini: cinnamon

Dava: medicine

Deepavali: Hindu day of light

Dharma: righteousness; social interaction; the natural tendencies of all things; cosmic divine law

Dhobiwala: washerman

Dhoti: men's 4 meter wraparound

Draupati: Queen married to the Pandavas; symbol of female virtue

Dupatta: (see Chuni)

Duryodhan: evil cousin of the Pandavas

Elaichi: cardamom,

Ganesh Chaturthi: Hindu god, Ganesh's birthday

Gori videsh: white foreigner

Grama seva: service to the village

Grihalakshmi: goddess of the home; wife

Grihasta: house holder; homeowner

Gunas: subtle energy properties; three constituents of creation; sattva, rajas, thamas

Homa: ritualistic fire

Japa: repetition of mantra or a holy name

Jata: a matted hair braid associated with Lord Shiva

Jubbah: lady's loose fitting garment

Kankanas: ankle bells worn by dancers

Karma: the universal law of action and reaction

Kisan: farmer

Kurta: men's shirt

Kriya: action; a school of yoga

Lakh: the numeric quantity 100,000

Lakshmi: goddess of wealth and prosperity associated with the home

Lal mirchi: hot red chili pepper

Lassie: buttermilk beverage

Loka samasta sukino bavantu: A universal Sanskrit prayer for happiness of all beings

Lungi: garment; short male wrap-around measuring apprx. 6'

Mahabharata: Hindu epic complied by Veda Vyasa Mahatmas: great souls

Mala: rosary used for prayer or japa

Manas: mind; the mind's lower function

Mandir: a temple

Manu: first man, synonymous with Adam; law maker

Matabhumi: mother land

Maya: illusion; God's creative power

Mosami: citrus fruit similar to an orange

Murali: a flute, often associated with Lord Krishna

Murti: sacred idol

Nag & Trishul: snake & trident; national defense missiles

Namaste: traditional Indian greeting to 'nama' = holy

Nandi: Lord Siva's bull; vehicle manufacture name or God within

Navaratri: Hindu Goddess festival lasting nine days

Naxal: a communist political movement

Padmasana: traditional cross-leg yoga posture Paneer: cottage cheese

Parivar: family

Pradushan: smog, pollution

Pranam: humble abeyance; a sign of respect usually with folded hands

Prema: spiritual love

Puja: religious service; Hindu ritual worship

Punjabi: man's outfit from Punjab

Raga: classical Indian melody

Raja: king

Raja yoga: a yoga school rooted in Patanjali's Yoga Sutra resulting in miraculous powers

Rishi: sage; a great saint

Rudraksha: woody acorns associated with Lord Shiva
Sadhus: holy men and women; wandering ascetics
Sanayasi: celibate renunciates
Sari: traditional female dress of 6 yards of fabric
Sathya: truth; that which never changes
Saunf: anise seed
Seva: selfless service
Shanti: peace
Sona ki chiriya: golden bird; syn. for India
Swami: a holy person who has achieved a high level of spiritual realization
Tandava: Shivas' dance of creation & transformation
Tapas: physical austerities associated with yoga practice
Thobe: full-length long sleeve gown worn by Arab men
Tilak: forehead marking usually of sandal paste, kumkum or ash; Vishnu symbol
Tirtham: santified liquid, such as water or milk, used in worship
Tortilla: Mexican flat bread made of corn
Vakil: an attorney
Vedas: four sacred scriptures that form the foundation of the Hindu religion
Vedanta: Vedic philosophy founded on Upanishads
Videsh: foreigner, usually Western
Yoga: union with God; spiritual science & practice
Zamindar: land owner

ॐ